OCR A Level
Chemistry A
Lab Book

Published by Pearson Education Limited, 80 Strand, London, WC2R 0RL.

www.pearsonschoolsandfecolleges.co.uk

Text © Pearson Education Limited 2017
Typeset and illustrated by Tech-Set Ltd Gateshead
Original illustrations © Pearson Education Limited 2015
Cover design by Pete Stratton
Cover photo/illustration © Shutterstock: Gontar

First published 2017

19 18 17
10 9 8 7 6 5 4 3 2 1

British Library Cataloguing in Publication Data
A catalogue record for this book is available from the British Library

ISBN 978 1 292 20027 9

Acknowledgements
The publishers would like to thank Gillian Lindsey and Mark Woods for their contributions to the text.

The publishers would also like to thank Karen Myers, Adelene Cogill and David Goodfellow for their work on the original Teacher Resource Pack.

Note from the publisher
Pearson has robust editorial processes, including answer and fact checks, to ensure the accuracy of the content in this publication, and every effort is made to ensure this publication is free of errors. We are, however, only human, and occasionally errors do occur. Pearson is not liable for any misunderstandings that arise as a result of errors in this publication, but it is our priority to ensure that the content is accurate. If you spot an error, please do contact us at resourcescorrections@pearson.com so we can make sure it is corrected.

Pearson

1   Calculating the formula of magnesium oxide

2   Investigating the reactions of bases, alkalis and carbonates with acids

3   Finding the relative atomic mass of an unknown metal by gas collection

4   Finding the relative molecular mass of washing soda by titration

5   Investigating halogen displacement reactions

6   Testing for halide ions

7   Calculating the enthalpy change for the reaction between zinc and copper sulfate using a direct method

8   The reaction between calcium carbonate and hydrochloric acid

9   The effect of temperature on the rate of a reaction

10 Investigating the qualitative effect of concentration on equilibrium

11 Investigating the qualitative effect of temperature on equilibrium

12 Eliminating water from cyclohexanol

13 Oxidising ethanol to ethanoic acid

14 Comparing the rates of hydrolysis of haloalkanes

15 Making a haloalkane

16 Construct electrochemical cells and measure cell potentials

17 Find the amount of iron in an iron tablet using redox titration

18 Use a clock reaction to determine a rate equation

19 Synthesise aspirin from 2-hydroxybenzoic acid

20 Measure an enthalpy change of solution

21 Perform ligand substitution reactions

22 Identify an unknown carbonyl compound using 2,4-dinitrophenylhydrazine

23 Follow the rate of the iodine–propanone reaction using a titrimetric method

24 Identify amino acids using thin layer and paper chromatography

25 Ester hydrolysis

26 Determine the activation energy for the reaction between bromide ions and bromate(V) ions

27 Generate acid–base curves using a datalogger

28 Determine K_a for a weak acid

29 Reactions of carboxylic acids

30 Analyse organic and inorganic unknowns

Practical activity group (PAG)	Techniques/skills covered (minimum)	Covered
1 Moles determination	• use of appropriate apparatus to record measurements of mass and volume of a gas, 1.2.2(a)	☐
2 Acid–base titration	• measurement of volume of a liquid, 1.2.2(a) • use of volumetric flask, including accurate technique for making up a standard solution, 1.2.2(e) • use of laboratory apparatus for titration using burette and pipette,1.2.2(d)(i) • use of acid–base indicators in titrations of weak/strong acids with weak/strong alkalis, 1.2.2(f)	☐ ☐ ☐ ☐
3 Enthalpy determination	• use of appropriate apparatus to record measurements of temperature, 1.2.2(a)	☐
4 Qualitative analysis of ions	• use of laboratory apparatus for qualitative tests for ions,1.2.2(d)(iii) • make and record qualitative observations,1.2.1(d)	☐
5 Synthesis of an organic liquid	• use of laboratory apparatus for heating under reflux, 1.2.2(d)(ii) • purification of a liquid product, including use of a separating funnel, 1.2.2(g)(ii) • use of laboratory apparatus for distillation,1.2.2(d)(ii) • identification of potential hazards (risk assessment), CPAC3	☐ ☐ ☐ ☐
6 Synthesis of an organic solid	• use of laboratory apparatus for heating under reflux, 1.2.2(d)(ii) • use of laboratory apparatus for filtration, including use of fluted filter paper, or filtration under reduced pressure, 1.2.2(d)(iv) • purification of a solid product by recrystallisation,1.2.2(g)(i) • use of melting point apparatus,1.2.2(h) • use of thin layer or paper chromatography,1.2.2(i) • identification of potential hazards (risk assessment), CPAC3	☐ ☐ ☐ ☐ ☐ ☐
7 Qualitative analysis of organic functional groups	• use of laboratory apparatus for qualitative tests for organic functional groups, 1.2.2(d)(iii) • use of a water bath or electric heater or sand bath for heating,1.2.2(b) • make and record qualitative observations,1.2.1(d)	☐ ☐
8 Electrochemical cells	• setting up of electrochemical cells and measuring voltages,1.2.2(j)	☐
9 Rates of reaction – continuous monitoring method	• measurement of rate of reaction by a continuous monitoring method, 1.2.2(l)(ii) • use of appropriate apparatus to record measurements of time,1.2.2(a) • use appropriate software to process data, 1.2.1(g)	☐ ☐ ☐
10 Rates of reaction – initial rates method	• measurement of rate of reaction by an initial rate method such as a clock reaction, 1.2.2(l)(i) • identify and control variables, CPAC2 • use appropriate software to process data, 1.2.1(g)	☐ ☐ ☐
11 pH measurement	• measurement of pH using pH charts, or pH meter, or pH probe on a data logger, 1.2.2(c)	☐
12 Research skills	• apply investigative approaches and methods to practical work, 1.2.1(a) • use online and offline research skills, including websites, textbooks and other printed scientific sources of information, 1.2.1(h) • correctly cite sources of information, 1.2.1(j)	☐ ☐ ☐

There is no practical endorsement (direct assessment of practical skills) for AS qualifications. However, students must be able to answer questions relating to practical work in the written papers at both AS and A level.

For A level students, assessment of practical skills can be carried out throughout the two-year course. In this Lab Book, practicals 1 to 15 cover first year work, while practicals 16 to 30 cover second year content. This book has practical activities across all the Practical Activity Groups (PAGs) in the specification. Some PAGs, however, lie within the content of the second year of the course.

In order to achieve a **pass** for the Practical Endorsement at A level, students will need to have completed a minimum of 12 practical activities from the Practical Activity Groups (PAGs) and to have met the expectations of the Common Practical Assessment Criteria (CPAC). Students will be expected to develop these competencies through the acquisition of the technical skills demonstrated in any practical activity undertaken throughout the course of study. The practical activities will provide opportunities for demonstrating competence in the skills identified, together with the use of apparatus and practical techniques.

Students may work in groups but must be able to demonstrate and record independent evidence of their competency. This must include evidence of independent application of investigative approaches and methods to practical work. Teachers who award a pass to their students need to be confident that the student consistently and routinely exhibits the competencies listed below before completion of the A level course.

While the Publishers have made every attempt to ensure that advice on the qualification and its assessment is accurate, the official specification and associated assessment guidance materials are the only authoritative source of information and should always be referred to for definitive guidance.

CPAC statements

1	Follows written procedures	**a)** Correctly follows instructions to carry out the experimental techniques or procedures.
2	Applies investigative approaches and methods when using instruments and equipment	**a)** Correctly uses appropriate instrumentation, apparatus and materials (including ICT) to carry out investigative activities, experimental techniques and procedures with minimal assistance or prompting. **b)** Carries out techniques or procedures methodically, in sequence and in combination, identifying practical issues and making adjustments when necessary. **c)** Identifies and controls significant quantitative variables where applicable, and plans approaches to take account of variables that cannot readily be controlled. **d)** Selects appropriate equipment and measurement strategies in order to ensure suitably accurate results.
3	Safely uses a range of practical equipment and materials	**a)** Identifies hazards and assesses risks associated with these hazards, making safety adjustments as necessary, when carrying out experimental techniques and procedures in the lab or field. **b)** Uses appropriate safety equipment and approaches to minimise risks with minimal prompting.
4	Makes and records observations	**a)** Makes accurate observations relevant to the experimental or investigative procedure. **b)** Obtains accurate, precise and sufficient data for experimental and investigative procedures and records this methodically using appropriate units and conventions.
5	Researches, references and reports	**a)** Uses appropriate software and/or tools to process data, carry out research and report findings. **b)** Sources of information are cited demonstrating that research has taken place, supporting planning and conclusions.

Core practical statements

Practical	Date	1a	2a	2b	2c	2d	3a	3b	4a	4b	5a	5b	Evidence/comment
1 Calculating the formula of magnesium oxide													
2 Investigating the reactions of bases, alkalis and carbonates with acids					▓	▓	▓	▓	▓			▓	
3 Finding the relative atomic mass of an unknown metal by gas collection					▓	▓				▓		▓	
4 Finding the relative molecular mass of washing soda by titration					▓	▓						▓	
5 Investigating halogen displacement reactions					▓	▓			▓			▓	
6 Testing for halide ions							▓						
7 Calculating the enthalpy change for the reaction between zinc and copper sulfate using a direct method					▓	▓	▓	▓	▓				
8 The reaction between calcium carbonate and hydrochloric acid					▓	▓			▓			▓	
9 The effect of temperature on the rate of a reaction					▓	▓			▓			▓	
10 Investigating the qualitative effect of concentration on equilibrium			▓		▓	▓						▓	
11 Investigating the qualitative effect of temperature on equilibrium			▓		▓	▓				▓	▓	▓	
12 Eliminating water from cyclohexanol					▓	▓			▓			▓	
13 Oxidising ethanol to ethanoic acid					▓	▓			▓			▓	
14 Comparing the rates of hydrolysis of haloalkanes					▓	▓						▓	
15 Making a haloalkane					▓	▓						▓	

Key: W – Working towards   Y – Criteria met   N – Criteria not met   A – Absent

Practical	Date	CPAC statements											Evidence/comment
		1a	2a	2b	2c	2d	3a	3b	4a	4b	5a	5b	
16 Construct electrochemical cells and measure cell potentials													
17 Find the amount of iron in an iron tablet using redox titration													
18 Use a clock reaction to determine a rate equation													
19 Synthesise aspirin from 2-hydroxybenzoic acid													
20 Measure an enthalpy change of solution													
21 Perform ligand substitution reactions													
22 Identify an unknown carbonyl compound using 2,4-dinitrophenylhydrazine													
23 Follow the rate of the iodine–propanone reaction using a titrimetric method													
24 Identify amino acids using thin layer and paper chromatography													
25 Ester hydrolysis													
26 Determine the activation energy for the reaction between bromide ions and bromate(V) ions													
27 Generate acid–base curves using a datalogger													
28 Determine K_a for a weak acid													
29 Reactions of carboxylic acids													
30 Analyse organic and inorganic unknowns													

Key: W – Working towards   Y – Criteria met   N – Criteria not met   A – Absent

PAG 1

CPAC links		Evidence	Done
1a	Correctly follows instructions to carry out the experimental techniques or procedures.	Practical observation	
2a	Correctly uses appropriate instrumentation, apparatus and materials (including ICT) to carry out investigative activities, experimental techniques and procedures with minimal assistance or prompting.	Practical observation	
2b	Carries out techniques or procedures methodically, in sequence and in combination, identifying practical issues and making adjustments when necessary.	Method followed	
2c	Identifies and controls significant quantitative variables where applicable, and plans approaches to take account of variables that cannot readily be controlled.	Plan	
2d	Selects appropriate equipment and measurement strategies in order to ensure suitably accurate results.	Plan	
3a	Identifies hazards and assesses risks associated with these hazards, making safety adjustments as necessary, when carrying out experimental techniques and procedures in the lab or field.	Risk assessment	
3b	Uses appropriate safety equipment and approaches to minimise risks with minimal prompting.	Risk assessment	
4a	Makes accurate observations relevant to the experimental or investigative procedure.	Results table	
4b	Obtains accurate, precise and sufficient data for experimental and investigative procedures and records this methodically using appropriate units and conventions.	Results table	
5a	Uses appropriate software and/or tools to process data, carry out research and report findings.	Calculation of formula	
5b	Sources of information are cited, demonstrating that research has taken place, supporting planning and conclusions.	Relevant references	

Objectives

- To calculate empirical formulae from element analysis data
- To perform calculations with reacting masses

Procedure

1   Find two sources that explain how the formula of magnesium oxide can be determined by heating magnesium using a practical method. Write down the references of both sources in an appropriate format.

2   Using this research, write a full method and risk assessment to explain how the formula of magnesium oxide can be determined by heating magnesium. Your plan must include:

-   a detailed risk assessment
-   details of any variables that need to be controlled
-   an equipment list including any reagents that you will need.

3   You must have your risk assessment and method checked before you begin any practical work.

Learning tips

-   To calculate the mass of magnesium, subtract the mass of the crucible without the magnesium ribbon in it, from the mass of the crucible with the magnesium ribbon in it.
-   The mass of oxygen can be calculated by subtracting the mass of the crucible and magnesium ribbon before heating from the mass of the crucible after heating.

Record your plan here, then get it checked.

-   Make sure you include an equipment list and risk assessment.
-   Remember to cite the sources of information.

Record your results here.

Analysis of results

Calculate the formula of the magnesium oxide produced. Show your working.

Questions

1 What is meant by the term empirical formula?

....

....

2 What is the empirical formula of magnesium oxide?

....

3 The relative mass of magnesium oxide is 40. What is its formula?

....

4 Write an equation for the reaction between magnesium and oxygen.

....

....

PAG 2

CPAC links		Evidence	Done
1a	Correctly follows instructions to carry out the experimental techniques or procedures.	Practical observation	
2a	Correctly uses appropriate instrumentation, apparatus and materials (including ICT) to carry out investigative activities, experimental techniques and procedures with minimal assistance or prompting.	Practical observation	
2b	Carries out techniques or procedures methodically, in sequence and in combination, identifying practical issues and making adjustments when necessary.	Method followed	
4b	Obtains accurate, precise and sufficient data for experimental and investigative procedures and records this methodically using appropriate units and conventions.	Results	
5a	Uses appropriate software and/or tools to process data, carry out research and report findings.	Equations and conclusions	

Objectives

- To recall the reactions between acids and bases
- To recall the reactions between acids and alkalis
- To appreciate the difference between strong acids and weak acids
- To know that neutralisation is the reaction between H^+ and OH^- to form H_2O
- To know the reactions of acids with bases including carbonates, metal oxides and alkalis (water soluble bases) to form salts, and to know the equations for these reactions

Equipment

- $1\,mol\,dm^{-3}$ hydrochloric acid (HCl)
- $0.5\,mol\,dm^{-3}$ sulfuric acid (H_2SO_4)
- $1\,mol\,dm^{-3}$ ethanoic acid (CH_3COOH)
- $1\,mol\,dm^{-3}$ citric acid ($C_6H_8O_7$)
- 1g copper oxide and 1g magnesium oxide
- $0.4\,mol\,dm^{-3}$ sodium hydroxide (NaOH) (alkali)
- $0.4\,mol\,dm^{-3}$ ammonia solution (NH_3) (alkali)
- 1g copper carbonate and 1g calcium carbonate
- $30\,cm^3$ limewater
- 24 boiling tubes and delivery tubes to fit
- spatula
- universal indicator
- $0–50 \times 0.2\,°C$ thermometer
- two $10\,cm^3$ measuring cylinders

Safety

- Wear eye protection.
- Acids are irritants.
- Alkalis are irritants at $0.4\,mol\,dm^{-3}$.
- Copper oxide and copper carbonate are harmful.

Irritant   Harmful

Procedure

Compare the reactivity of the four acids with the metal oxide bases (copper oxide and magnesium oxide).

1 Take eight boiling tubes. Place $5\,cm^3$ of acid in each boiling tube – two tubes for each acid.

2 Add a small amount of copper oxide to one boiling tube for each acid. Add a small amount of magnesium oxide to the other boiling tube for each acid.

3 Observe the reactions of the acids and the bases and record your results in the space on the next page. You may need to warm the mixtures before you see a reaction.

Compare the reactivity of the four acids with the alkalis (sodium hydroxide and ammonia solution).

1 Take eight boiling tubes. Place $5\,cm^3$ of acid in each boiling tube – two tubes for each acid.

2 Add $5\,cm^3$ of sodium hydroxide to one boiling tube for each acid. Add $5\,cm^3$ of ammonia solution to the other boiling tube for each acid.

3 Monitor any temperature changes in the boiling tubes and record your results in the space on the next page.

4 Now add a few drops of universal indicator followed by excess alkali to each boiling tube. Record your observations.

Compare the reactivity of the four acids with the metal carbonates (copper carbonate and calcium carbonate).

1 Take eight boiling tubes. Fill four boiling tubes to a 1 cm depth with copper carbonate. Fill the other four boiling tubes to a 1 cm depth with calcium carbonate.

2 Add each acid to one boiling tube containing each of the carbonates.

3 Pass any gas produced through limewater. Record your observations.

Learning tips

- Know the names and formulae of the common acids and alkalis.
- You should be able to write balanced equations for the reactions of acids with oxides, alkalis and carbonates.
- Know that an acid is a hydrogen ion, H^+ (proton), donor.
- Know that a base is a hydrogen ion, H^+ (proton), acceptor.
- Know that an alkali forms hydroxide ions, OH^-, in water.

Record your results and observations here.

Analysis of results

- Record your observations in an appropriate format in the space above.
- Write an equation for each reaction.

....

....

....

....

....

....

....

....

....

....

- Compare the reactivity of the acids and relate this to their strength.

....

....

....

....

- Comment on any anomalous observations.

....

....

....

....

Questions

1   The temperature rises in the second set of boiling tubes are caused by the exothermic reaction:

   $H^+ + OH^- \rightarrow H_2O$

   Explain why the reactions do not all give the same temperature rise, even though the same amounts of acid and alkali are used.

....

....

....

....

2   Sodium hydroxide is used in oven cleaners because it reacts with fats. Suggest why $0.4 \, mol \, dm^{-3}$ alkali solution is used in this experiment, rather than $1 \, mol \, dm^{-3}$.

....

....

....

3   Hydrochloric acid is present in the stomach. Suggest which compounds would be suitable for neutralising excess stomach acidity.

....

....

....

4   Wasp stings are alkaline. Name a household substance that could be used to reduce the pain of a wasp sting. Give a reason for your answer.

....

....

CPAC links		Evidence	Done
1a	Correctly follows instructions to carry out the experimental techniques or procedures.	Practical observation	
2a	Correctly uses appropriate instrumentation, apparatus and materials (including ICT) to carry out investigative activities, experimental techniques and procedures with minimal assistance or prompting.	Practical observation	
2b	Carries out techniques or procedures methodically, in sequence and in combination, identifying practical issues and making adjustments when necessary.	Method followed	
5a	Uses appropriate software and/ or tools to process data, carry out research and report findings.	Identity of X, based on value of A_r	

Diagram

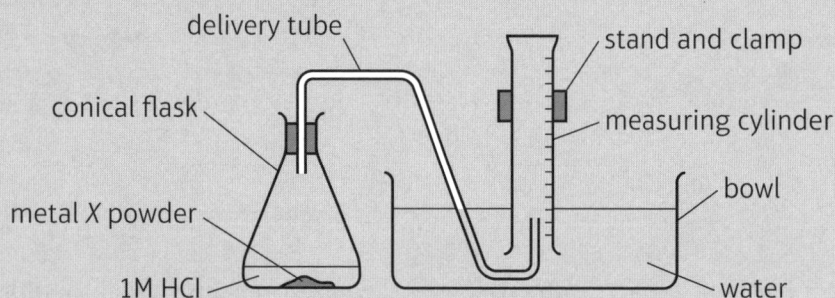

Figure A. Apparatus for finding the relative atomic mass of an unknown metal by gas collection

Procedure

1 Set up your apparatus as shown in Figure A. Fill the measuring cylinder with water, cover the open end and support this with the clamp. Make sure the open end of the measuring cylinder is under the water in the bowl.

2 Put between 0.15 g and 0.20 g of the unknown metal, X, into the conical flask.

3 Measure 25 cm^3 of hydrochloric acid and pour this directly into the conical flask, as quickly as possible. Connect the delivery tube to the flask immediately afterwards.

4 Ensure that all the metal reacts.

5 Collect the gas and record the final volume of hydrogen in the measuring cylinder.

Learning tips

- Record the measured mass of X and the volume of gas collected before you begin your calculations.
- Explain each line of your calculation as shown in the Analysis of results section.
- Consider how many significant figures to use during your calculation.
- Consider how many significant figures to use in your final answer.

Objectives

- To collect a gas from a reaction
- To measure the volume of a gas
- To calculate relative atomic mass
- To perform calculations using the amounts of substances in moles, involving mass and gas volume
- To know the techniques required during experiments involving the measurement of gas volumes

Equipment

- 1 mol dm^{-3} hydrochloric acid
- unknown metal, X
- weighing bottle
- mass balance (2 d.p.)
- 250 cm^3 conical flask
- delivery tube
- 250 cm^3 measuring cylinder
- stand and clamp
- bowl
- 25 cm^3 measuring cylinder

Safety

- Wear eye protection.
- Unknown metal is flammable.
- Hydrogen gas is flammable.
- No naked flames.
- 1 mol dm^{-3} hydrochloric acid (low hazard) may harm eyes or irritate cuts.

Flammable

Record your results here.

Analysis of results

- Calculate the number of moles of hydrogen collected.

    One mole of gas occupies $24\,000\,cm^3$ at room temperature and pressure (298 K and 101 kPa).

    ....

    ....

    ....

    ....

- The equation for the reaction is:

    $X + 2HCl \rightarrow XCl_2 + H_2$

    Use this equation to calculate the number of moles of the unknown metal used.

    ....

    ....

    ....

    ....

- Calculate the relative atomic mass, A_r, of X.

    ....

    ....

    ....

    ....

- Suggest an identity for X, based on your value of A_r and its observed reactivity.

    ....

    ....

    ....

Questions

1 State one major procedural error in this experiment.

    ....

    ....

    ....

    ....

2 Suggest a modification that would reduce this error.

    ....

    ....

    ....

3 Calculate the number of moles of each reactant (using your value of A_r for X) to confirm that the acid was in excess.

....

....

....

....

....

....

....

....

....

....

4 How would you modify the procedure if metal X was provided in lump form?

....

....

....

....

....

....

....

5 How could this experiment be modified to measure the relative atomic mass of lithium?

....

....

....

....

....

....

....

....

PAG 2

CPAC links		Evidence	Done
1a	Correctly follows instructions to carry out the experimental techniques or procedures.	Practical observation	
2a	Correctly uses appropriate instrumentation, apparatus and materials (including ICT) to carry out investigative activities, experimental techniques and procedures with minimal assistance or prompting.	Practical observation	
2b	Carries out techniques or procedures methodically, in sequence and in combination, identifying practical issues and making adjustments when necessary.	Results table	
4a	Makes accurate observations relevant to the experimental or investigative procedure.	Teacher check of burette reading	
4b	Obtains accurate, precise and sufficient data for experimental and investigative procedures and records this methodically using appropriate units and conventions.	Results table	
5a	Uses appropriate software and/or tools to process data, carry out research and report findings.	Calculations	

Procedure

1   Put approximately 2.65 g of anhydrous sodium carbonate in a beaker and weigh it accurately.

2   Make a standard solution by dissolving the anhydrous sodium carbonate in deionised or distilled water (from the wash bottle) and make it up to the mark in the 250 cm³ volumetric flask. Label the flask.

3   Fill the burette with hydrochloric acid.

4   Pipette 25 cm³ of the standard sodium carbonate solution into a conical flask and titrate it with the hydrochloric acid. Use methyl orange as the indicator.

5   Repeat step 4 until concordant titres are obtained. Record your results in a suitable table.

   Have one of your burette readings checked by your teacher.

Learning tips

• It is important to present your results (with units) in a table showing the initial and final burette readings.

• Show clearly how the average titre is obtained.

• Explain each line of your calculation.

• Consider how many significant figures to use during your calculation.

• Consider how many significant figures to use in your final answer.

Objectives

• To be able to make a standard solution

• To be able to carry out a titration using volumetric equipment

• To be able to calculate relative molecular mass using moles

• To be able to carry out structured and non-structured titration calculations

Equipment

• eye protection

• anhydrous sodium carbonate (Na_2CO_3)

• methyl orange

• 0.2 mol dm⁻³ hydrochloric acid (HCl)

• 25 cm³ pipette and pipette filler

• 50 cm³ burette

• stand

• white tile

• 250 cm³ volumetric flask

• weighing bottle

• beaker

• stirring rod

• funnel

• 250 cm³ conical flask

• spatula

• mass balance (2 d.p.)

• label

• wash bottle

Safety

• Wear eye protection.

• Ensure that burettes are filled with the top of the burette below eye level.

• Sodium carbonate is alkaline and an irritant.

Irritant

Record your results here.

Analysis of results

- Calculate the concentration of the standard solution, using the original mass of sodium carbonate.

....

....

....

....

- $25\,cm^3$ of standard sodium carbonate solution was pipetted into the conical flask. Calculate the number of moles of sodium carbonate pipetted into the flask.

....

....

....

....

- The equation for the reaction is:

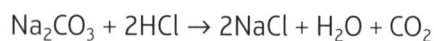

    $Na_2CO_3 + 2HCl \rightarrow 2NaCl + H_2O + CO_2$

    Use your answer from the previous question and the equation above to calculate the number of moles of HCl used.

....

....

....

....

- Using concordant results, calculate the average titre, in cm^3, of the hydrochloric acid.

....

....

....

- Calculate the concentration of the hydrochloric acid.

....

....

....

Questions

1 How did you eliminate procedural errors when making the standard solution?

....

....

....

....

2 If your pipette, burette and conical flask are dirty, you will need to rinse them before you use them. What would you use to rinse each one?

....

....

....

....

....

3 What do you think was the main procedural error when carrying out the titration? What did you do to try to eliminate this?

....

....

....

....

....

....

4 To calculate precision errors, you use the equation:

$$\% \text{ uncertainty} = \frac{\text{uncertainty}}{\text{reading}} \times 100$$

The uncertainty associated with a 25 cm^3 pipette is 0.06 cm^3. Calculate the percentage uncertainty of your pipette reading.

....

....

....

....

....

5 The uncertainty associated with a burette reading is 0.05 cm^3. Calculate the percentage uncertainty of your burette reading.

....

....

....

....

PAG 4

CPAC links		Evidence	Done
1a	Correctly follows instructions to carry out the experimental techniques or procedures.	Practical observation	
2a	Correctly uses appropriate instrumentation, apparatus and materials (including ICT) to carry out investigative activities, experimental techniques and procedures with minimal assistance or prompting.	Practical observation	
2b	Carries out techniques or procedures methodically, in sequence and in combination, identifying practical issues and making adjustments when necessary.	Method followed	
4b	Obtains accurate, precise and sufficient data for experimental and investigative procedures and records this methodically using appropriate units and conventions.	Table of results	
5a	Uses appropriate software and/or tools to process data, carry out research and report findings.	Equations and conclusions	

Objectives

- To compare halogen reactivity using displacement
- To extract halogens into an organic solvent
- To know the trend in reactivity of the halogens, as illustrated by their reactions with other halide ions

Equipment

- $1\,mol\,dm^{-3}$ potassium chloride
- $1\,mol\,dm^{-3}$ potassium bromide
- $1\,mol\,dm^{-3}$ potassium iodide
- chlorine water
- bromine water
- iodine solution
- cyclohexane
- six test tubes with stoppers
- test tube rack
- dropping pipette

Safety

- Wear eye protection.
- Dispense halogens from a fume cupboard.
- Test tubes should be fitted with stoppers when taken out of the fume cupboard.
- Cyclohexane is harmful and highly flammable.
- Do not inhale gases.

Toxic   Harmful   Flammable

Diagram

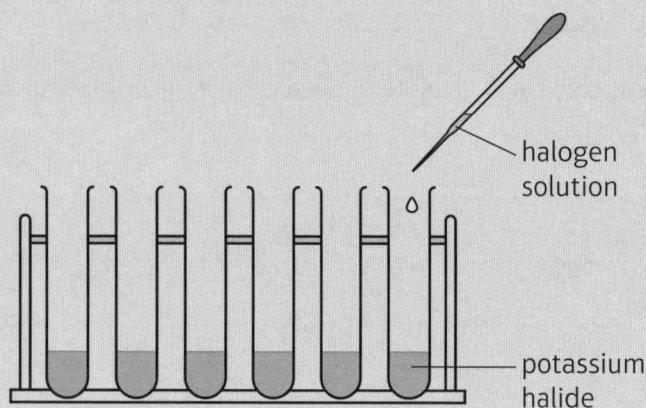

Figure A. Investigating halogen displacement reactions

Procedure

1. Pour one of the potassium halide solutions into a test tube to a depth of 2 cm.

2. Add an equal volume of a different halogen solution.

3. Put a stopper in the test tube and shake carefully.

4. Remove the stopper and add an equal volume of cyclohexane.

5. Replace the stopper in the test tube and shake carefully.

6. Record all observations.

7. Repeat steps 1–5 for each of the different combinations of potassium halide and halogen solution.

Learning tips

- Look for patterns in your results.
- Relate these patterns to the order of the group 17 halogens.
- Explain any patterns in terms of the ability of halogens to gain an electron.
- Make sure you can write balanced chemical equations, with state symbols, as well as word equations.

Record your results here.

Analysis of results

- Cl_2 is yellow/green in cyclohexane.
- Br_2 is orange in cyclohexane.
- I_2 is purple in cyclohexane.
- Use this information to interpret your results and to decide what reactions have occurred.

....

....

....

....

....

....

- Write equations for any reactions observed. The following equations will help you:

$Cl_2 + 2KBr \rightarrow Br_2 + 2KCl$

$Cl_2 + 2KI \rightarrow I_2 + 2KCl$

$Br_2 + 2KI \rightarrow I_2 + 2KBr$

....

....

....

....

....

- Once you have analysed your results, write the halogens in order of decreasing reactivity.

....

Questions

1   Place the halogens in order of their ability to gain an electron.

....

2   Explain the order of ability of halogens to gain an electron, in terms of atomic radius and nuclear charge.

....

....

....

....

3   Write the equation for the reaction between chlorine and potassium iodide, with state symbols.

....

....

4   Write the ionic equation for the reaction between chlorine and potassium iodide.

....

....

5   Predict the reaction, if any, between:

   a chlorine and potassium astatide

....

....

   b astatine and potassium iodide.

....

....

PAG **4**

CPAC links		Evidence	Done
1a	Correctly follows instructions to carry out the experimental techniques or procedures.	Practical observation	
2a	Correctly uses appropriate instrumentation, apparatus and materials (including ICT) to carry out investigative activities, experimental techniques and procedures with minimal assistance or prompting.	Practical observation	
2b	Carries out techniques or procedures methodically, in sequence and in combination, identifying practical issues and making adjustments when necessary.	Method followed	
2c	Identifies and controls significant quantitative variables where applicable, and plans approaches to take account of variables that cannot readily be controlled.	Plan	
2d	Selects appropriate equipment and measurement strategies in order to ensure suitably accurate results.	Plan	
3a	Identifies hazards and assesses risks associated with these hazards, making safety adjustments as necessary, when carrying out experimental techniques and procedures in the lab or field.	Risk assessment	
3b	Uses appropriate safety equipment and approaches to minimise risks with minimal prompting.	Risk assessment	
4a	Makes accurate observations relevant to the experimental or investigative procedure.	Accuracy of results	
4b	Obtains accurate, precise and sufficient data for experimental and investigative procedures and records this methodically using appropriate units and conventions.	Results	
5a	Uses appropriate software and/ or tools to process data, carry out research and report findings.	Results and conclusions	
5b	Sources of information are cited demonstrating that research has taken place, supporting planning and conclusions.	Relevant references	

Objectives

- To know the precipitation reactions of the aqueous anions Cl^-, Br^- and I^-, with aqueous silver ions followed by ammonia, and to know the ionic equations for these reactions
- To carry out qualitative analysis of halide ions on a test tube scale

Equipment

- Three unknown solutions: A, B and C

Procedure

1 Find two sources that explain how halide ions can be identified using a practical method. Write down the references of both sources in an appropriate format.

2 Using this research, write a full method and risk assessment for an experiment to identify three unknown solutions of chloride, bromide and iodide ions in the space provided. Your plan must include:

- a detailed risk assessment
- details of any variables that need to be controlled
- an equipment list including any reagents that you will need.

3 You must have your risk assessment and method checked before you begin any practical work.

Learning tips

- Look for differences in the tests that make them unique and, hence, make them useful as definitive tests.
- Write balanced chemical equations for the reactions.

Record your plan here, then get it checked.

- Make sure you include an equipment list and risk assessment.
- Remember to cite the sources of information.

Record your results, and present them in a table, here.

Analysis of results

● Present your results in a table.

● Write equations for the precipitation reactions.

....

....

....

● Summarise your results by writing out the tests that are used to distinguish the three halide ions from each other.

....

....

....

....

....

....

Questions

1   Write equations for the reactions of silver nitrate with potassium chloride, bromide and iodide, including the colours of the precipitates formed. State the solubility of the precipitates formed in dilute and concentrated ammonia.

....

....

....

....

....

....

2   What type of bonding would you expect in silver chloride? Explain your answer.

....

....

3   Explain why nitric acid rather than hydrochloric acid or sulfuric acid should be used in step 5 of the procedure.

....

....

4   Explain why tap water should not be used in step 5 of the procedure.

....

....

PAG 3

CPAC links		Evidence	Done
1a	Correctly follows instructions to carry out the experimental techniques or procedures.	Practical observation	
2a	Correctly uses appropriate instrumentation, apparatus and materials (including ICT) to carry out investigative activities, experimental techniques and procedures with minimal assistance or prompting.	Practical observation	
2b	Carries out techniques or procedures methodically, in sequence and in combination, identifying practical issues and making adjustments when necessary.	Method followed	
4a	Makes accurate observations relevant to the experimental or investigative procedure.	Accuracy of results	
4b	Obtains accurate, precise and sufficient data for experimental and investigative procedures and records this methodically using appropriate units and conventions.	Results and graph	
5a	Uses appropriate software and/ or tools to process data, carry out research and report findings.	Results and calculations	
5b	Sources of information are cited demonstrating that research has taken place, supporting planning and conclusions.	Relevant references	

Objectives

- To use a graph to ascertain a temperature change
- To calculate enthalpy changes directly from appropriate experimental results, including using the equation $q = mc\Delta T$

Equipment

- $200\,g\,dm^{-3}$ hydrated copper sulfate, $CuSO_4 \cdot 5H_2O$
- zinc powder
- mass balance (2 d.p.)
- weighing bottle
- polystyrene cup (reaction vessel)
- $0-100\,°C \times 0.5\,°C$ thermometer
- spatula
- stop clock
- $25\,cm^3$ pipette
- pipette filler
- stirring rod
- graph paper

Safety

- Zinc powder is flammable.
- Wear eye protection.
- Copper sulfate is harmful.

Flammable   Harmful

Procedure

1. Weigh an empty weighing bottle.

2. Weigh accurately between 2.9 g and 3 g of zinc powder in a weighing bottle. Record the mass of the weighing bottle plus the zinc.

3. Pour $25\,cm^3$ of the copper sulfate solution into the polystyrene cup.

4. Start the stop clock and record the temperature of the solution every 30 seconds for 2.5 minutes (2 minutes 30 seconds).

5. At exactly 3 minutes, add the zinc and stir the mixture thoroughly.

6. Record the temperature every 30 seconds from 3 minutes 30 seconds to 10 minutes, stirring thoroughly.

7. Reweigh the weighing bottle.

Learning tips

- The appropriate way to record your results is in a table.
- You need to be able to calculate amounts in moles and establish which substance is in excess.

- The concentration of the copper sulfate is 0.012 mol dm^{-3}.
- Enthalpy of reaction is measured per mole, as in the balanced equation.
- Take care with units. The symbol for kilojoules contains a lowercase k and a capital J.
- Similarly, 'per mole' is mol^{-1}, not /mol^{-1} or m^{-1}.
- Consider the accuracy of your data before deciding how many significant figures to use for the answer.

Record your results here.

Analysis of results

- Record your observations in an appropriate form.
- Plot a graph of temperature against time.

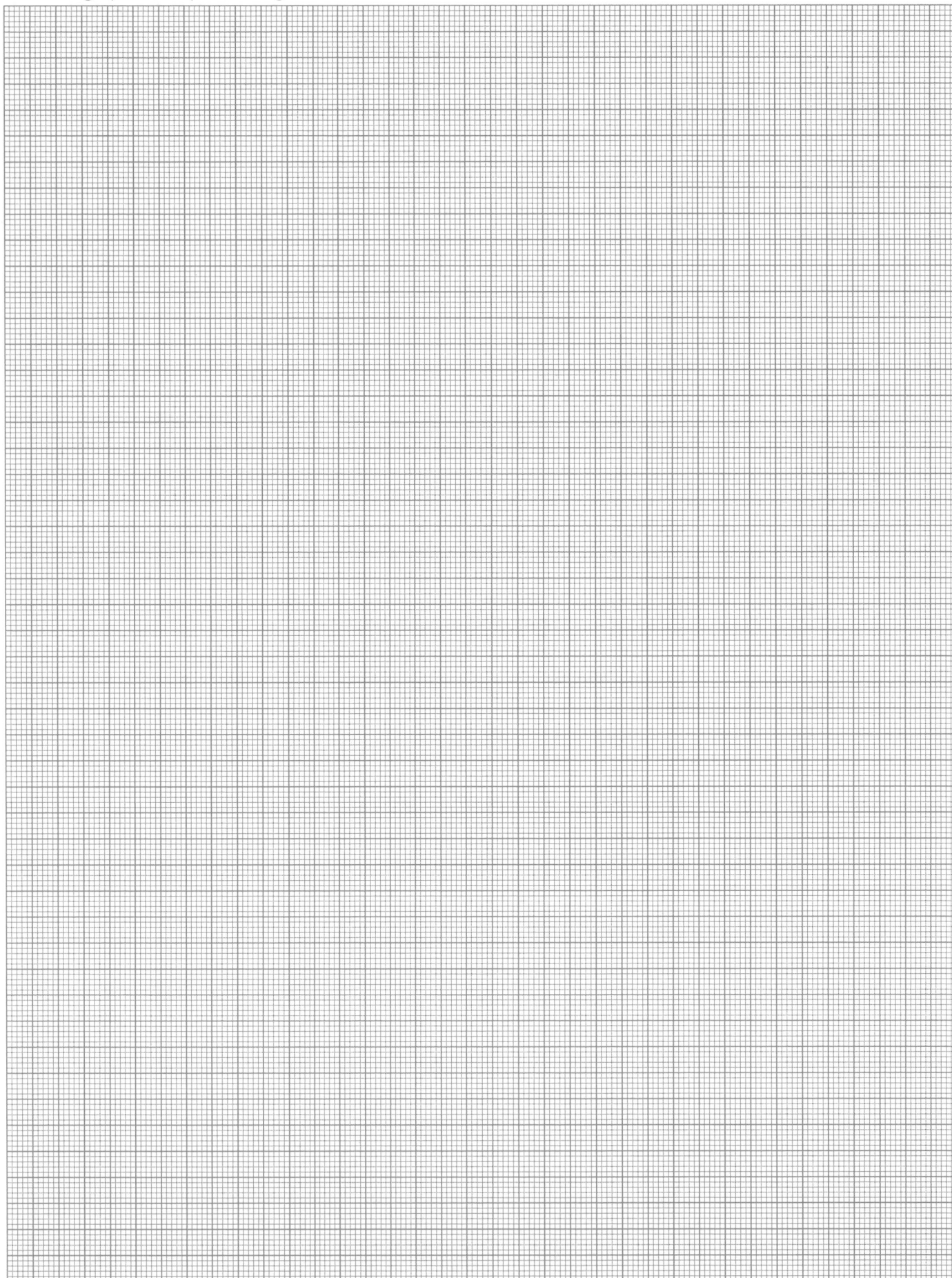

- Extrapolate the graph from the first five points to obtain the temperature at three minutes.

....

- Use the graph to find the temperature change during the reaction.

....

- Write an equation for the reaction.

....

- Calculate which substance is in excess and, hence, the number of moles reacting.

....

....

....

- Calculate the enthalpy change of the reaction.

....

....

....

- Look up the theoretical value of the enthalpy change from two different sources and suggest reasons why your answer differs from the theoretical value. Cite your references in an appropriate format.

....

....

....

....

....

....

....

Questions

1   Explain why the weighing bottle is weighed after the experiment.

....

....

2   What are the advantages and disadvantages of using a graph to find a temperature change?

....

....

....

3   What might be the most significant procedural error? Suggest a modification to the procedure to limit the effects of this error.

....

....

....

....

....

....

4   Calculate the possible measurement errors in this practical.

....

....

....

....

....

....

....

....

....

....

5   Explain, in terms of bonding, the source of the enthalpy change.

....

....

....

....

....

....

....

....

....

PAG 1

CPAC links		Evidence	Done
1a	Correctly follows instructions to carry out the experimental techniques or procedures.	Practical observation	
2a	Correctly uses appropriate instrumentation, apparatus and materials (including ICT) to carry out investigative activities, experimental techniques and procedures with minimal assistance or prompting.	Practical observation	
2b	Carries out techniques or procedures methodically, in sequence and in combination, identifying practical issues and making adjustments when necessary.	Method followed	
4b	Obtains accurate, precise and sufficient data for experimental and investigative procedures and records this methodically using appropriate units and conventions.	Results and graph	
5a	Uses appropriate software and/or tools to process data, carry out research and report findings.	Tangents and rate calculations	

Objectives

- To generate data that can be processed to produce a graph
- To calculate the reaction rate from the gradient of a graph, measuring how a physical quantity changes with time

Equipment

- $20\,cm^3$ of $0.5\,mol\,dm^{-3}$ hydrochloric acid
- $10\,g$ marble (medium-sized lumps)
- test tube with side-arm and stopper
- $100\,cm^3$ gas syringe
- two stands, clamps and bosses
- $100\,cm^3$ measuring cylinder
- stop clock
- $250\,cm^3$ conical flask
- cotton wool
- mass balance (2 d.p.)

Safety

- Wear eye protection.
- $0.5\,mol\,dm^{-3}$ hydrochloric acid (low hazard) may harm eyes and irritate cuts.

Diagram

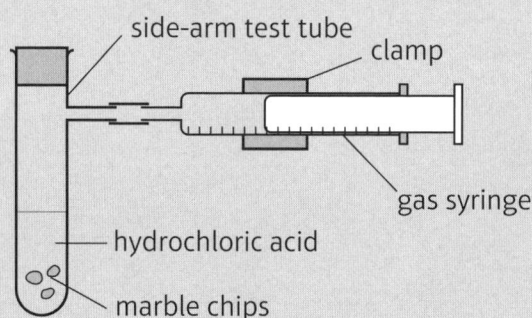

Figure A. Apparatus to investigate the reaction between calcium carbonate and hydrochloric acid

Procedure

Choose method 1 or 2.

Method 1

1 Measure $20\,cm^3$ of hydrochloric acid solution using a $100\,cm^3$ measuring cylinder.
2 Carefully pour the measured solution into a test tube with a side-arm and attach the side-arm to the gas syringe, as shown in the diagram.
3 Weigh out $10\,g$ of the marble chips. Make sure the pieces are approximately the same size.
4 Drop the marble chips into the acid.
5 Put the stopper in the test tube and start the stop clock at the same time. Note the volume of gas in the gas syringe. Do not shake the test tube.
6 Record the volume of gas collected every 30 seconds. Continue until the volume of gas remains constant.

Method 2

1 Weigh out 10 g of the marble chips. Make sure the pieces are approximately the same size.
2 Measure 20 cm^3 of hydrochloric acid solution using a 100 cm^3 measuring cylinder.
3 Carefully pour the measured solution into a conical flask and stand the flask on a mass balance.
4 Drop the marble chips into the flask and stuff cotton wool loosely into the mouth of the flask to prevent acid spray.
5 Start the stop clock and note the combined mass of the flask and the reactants.
6 Record the mass every 10 seconds for two minutes and then every 30 seconds, until the mass remains constant.

Learning tips

- Assess the reliability and accuracy of this experimental task. Identify significant weaknesses in experimental procedures and measurements.
- Understand and select simple improvements to experimental procedures and measurements.

Record your results here.

Analysis of results

- Plot a graph showing:
  - amount of gas produced against time (if you used Method 1); or
  - loss of mass against time (if you used Method 2).

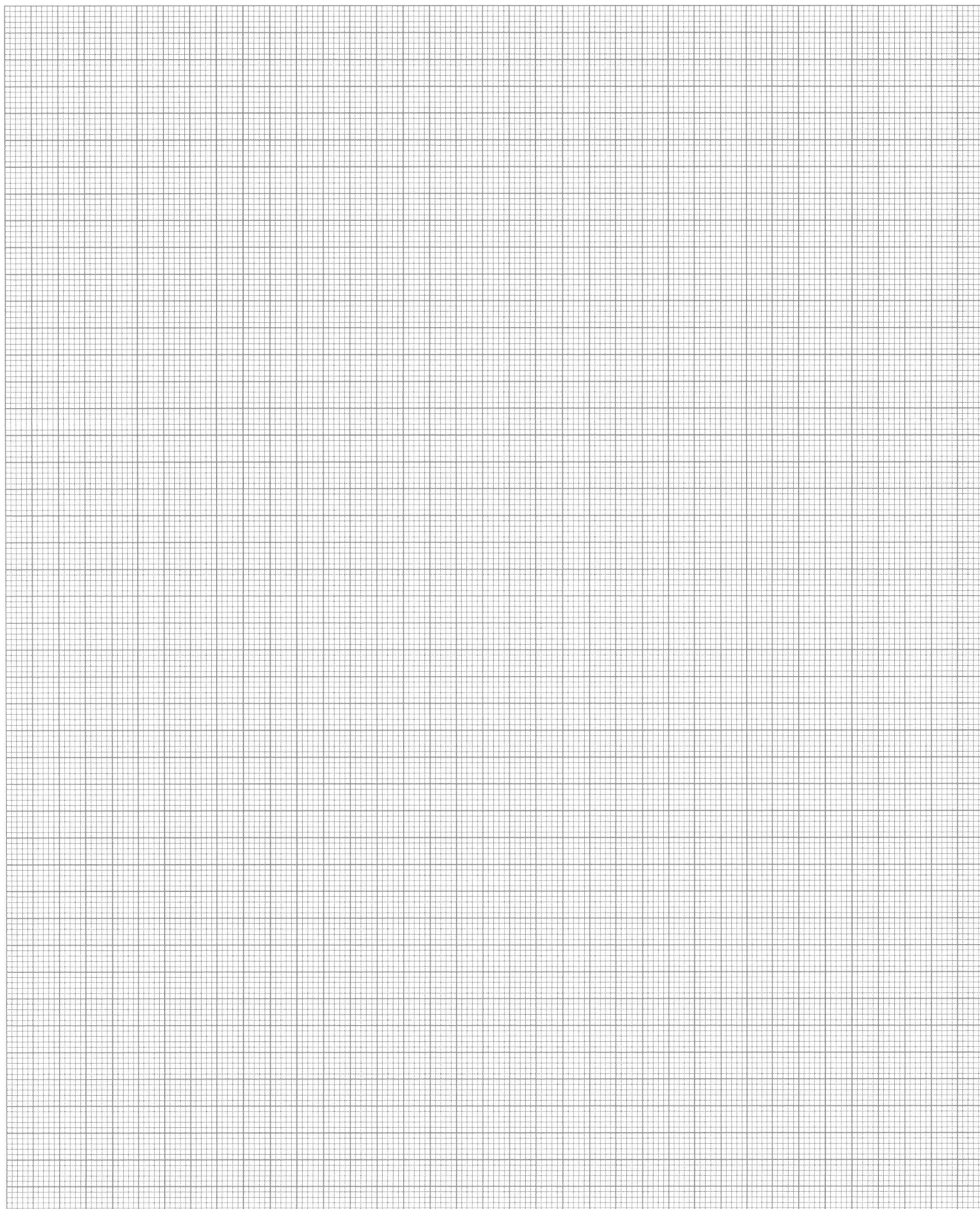

- A gradient of the curve is equal to the reaction rate at that time. Draw tangents to the curve to calculate the initial rate of reaction and the rate at two other times.

Questions

1   What might be the most significant procedural error? Suggest a modification for this.

....

....

....

....

....

....

....

....

....

2   Calculate the possible measurement errors in this practical.

....

....

....

....

....

....

....

....

....

3   What is the rate equation for this experiment?

....

....

4   Why is $[CaCO_3]$ not involved in the rate equation?

....

....

....

5   Use the rate equation to write an equation for the rate-determining step of this reaction.

....

....

PAG 3

CPAC links		Evidence	Done
1a	Correctly follows instructions to carry out the experimental techniques or procedures.	Practical observation	
2a	Correctly uses appropriate instrumentation, apparatus and materials (including ICT) to carry out investigative activities, experimental techniques and procedures with minimal assistance or prompting.	Practical observation	
2b	Carries out techniques or procedures methodically, in sequence and in combination, identifying practical issues and making adjustments when necessary.	Method followed	
4b	Obtains accurate, precise and sufficient data for experimental and investigative procedures and records this methodically using appropriate units and conventions.	Results and graph	
5a	Uses appropriate software and/ or tools to process data, carry out research and report findings.	Results and conclusions	

Objectives

- To calculate reaction rate from the gradient of a graph, measuring how a physical quantity changes over time
- To know how concentration affects the rate of a chemical reaction
- To know the techniques that can be used to investigate reaction rates

Equipment

- 150 cm^3 of 0.1 mol dm^{-3} sodium thiosulfate
- 150 cm^3 of 0.1 mol dm^{-3} hydrochloric acid
- two boiling tubes
- six 100 cm^3 conical flasks
- two 25 cm^3 measuring cylinders
- stop clock
- two thermometers (−10 to 110 °C)
- water bath
- filter paper with a cross marked in the centre
- hot/boiling water

Safety

- Perform the experiments in a well-ventilated laboratory because sulfur dioxide is toxic.
- Asthma sufferers should be particularly careful of the sulfur dioxide gas given off.
- Hydrochloric acid should not be heated above 55 °C.
- Do not operate a gas syringe when connected to a flask.
- Wear eye protection.

Toxic   Flammable

Procedure

Throughout this experiment, one boiling tube can be used for the sodium thiosulfate solution and the other can be used for the hydrochloric acid solution.

1 Measure and pour 10 cm^3 of sodium thiosulfate into one of the boiling tubes.

2 Measure and pour 10 cm^3 of hydrochloric acid into the other boiling tube.

3 Record the temperature of each solution.

4 Stand the conical flask on some filter paper so the cross can be seen clearly from above.

5 Pour the sodium thiosulfate solution into the conical flask.

6 Add the hydrochloric acid solution to the conical flask and start the stop clock.

7 Stop timing when the cross on the filter paper is completely obscured by the precipitate. Record the time taken.

Now repeat the experiment at several different temperatures between room temperature and 55 °C. You will need at least six different sets of readings. For each temperature:

8 Repeat steps 1 and 2, then place both boiling tubes in a water bath. Allow the solutions in both boiling tubes to reach the same temperature, and record the temperature of each solution.

9 Repeat steps 4–7 with the heated solutions.

Learning tips

- The appropriate format for your results is a table.
- Record your measurements to an appropriate precision.
- Interpret your experimental results to reach valid conclusions.
- Assess the accuracy of the task.

Record your results here.

Analysis of results

- Work out the average time for each temperature used.

....

....

....

....

....

....

- Use the average time to work out the average rate of reaction at that temperature.
  Calculate the rate using:
  $$\text{rate} = \frac{1}{\text{time}}$$

....

....

....

....

....

- Plot a graph of rate against temperature. What conclusions can you draw from the shape of your graph?

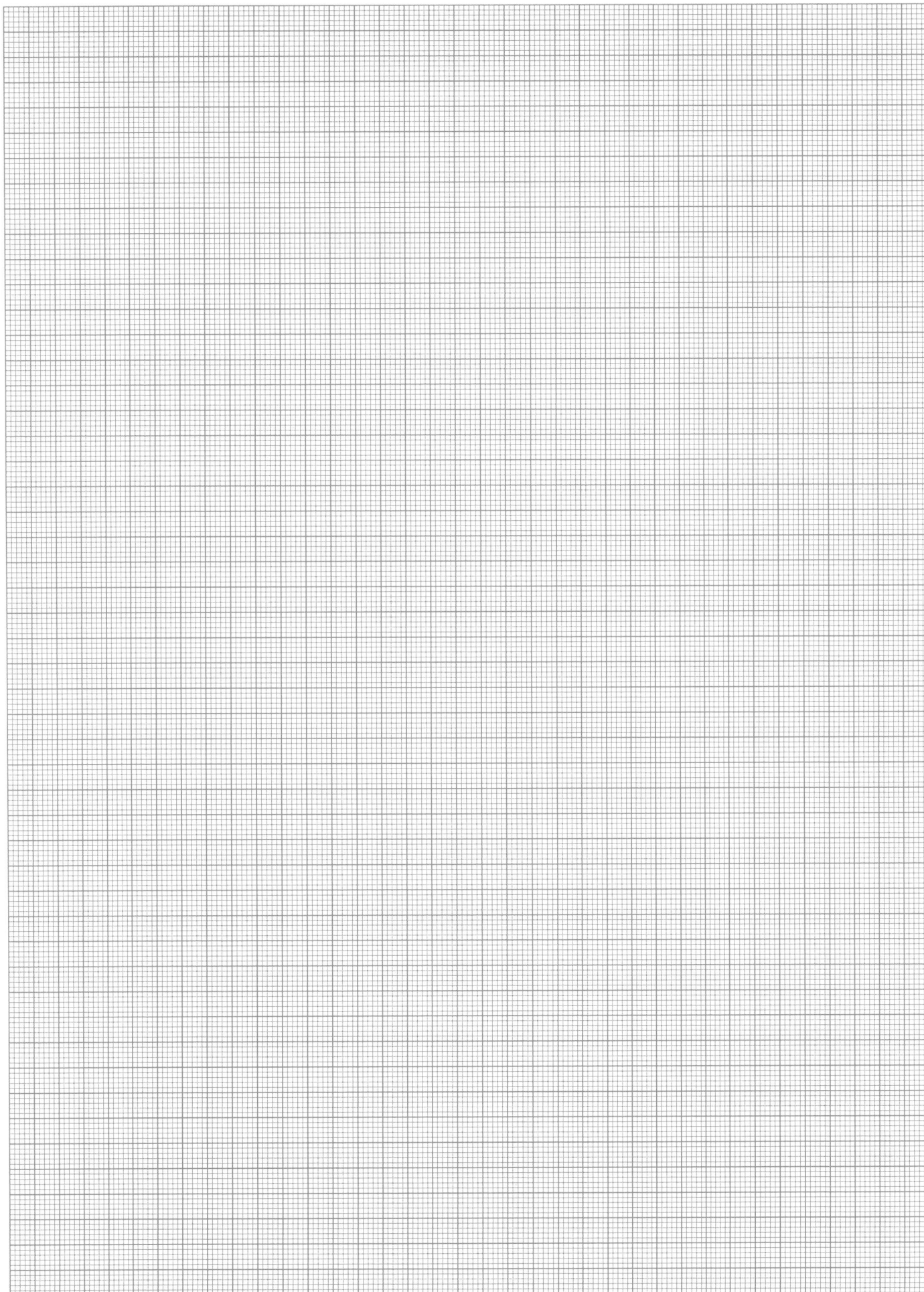

Questions

1   Identify the main procedural error in this experiment and suggest a way of improving it.

....

....

....

....

....

....

2   Identify the main measurement error and suggest a way of improving it.

....

....

....

....

....

....

3   How could you improve the reliability of the experiment?

....

....

....

....

....

4   Describe the effect that increasing temperature has on the rate of this reaction.

....

....

....

....

....

....

Practical 10 Investigating the qualitative effect of concentration on equilibrium

OCR A Level
Chemistry A

PAG 5

CPAC links		Evidence	Done
1a	Correctly follows instructions to carry out the experimental techniques or procedures.	Practical procedure	
2b	Carries out techniques or procedures methodically, in sequence and in combination, identifying practical issues and making adjustments when necessary.	Practical procedure	
3b	Uses appropriate safety equipment and approaches to minimise risks with minimal prompting.	Practical procedure	
4a	Makes accurate observations relevant to the experimental or investigative procedure.	Observations and answers to questions	

Procedure

1 Add 2 cm³ of iron(III) chloride solution to each of the five boiling tubes.

2 Add different volumes of potassium thiocyanate (KCNS) and water to each boiling tube, to make up five solutions, each with a volume of 20 cm³. You should now have five boiling tubes, each containing 20 cm³ of KCNS solution, with a different concentration in each tube.

3 Record the volume of each substance added to each boiling tube.

4 Observe the colour of each solution.

5 If necessary, repeat the experiment by making up other solutions using different concentrations of KCNS.

Learning tips

- An equilibrium must be represented using reversible arrows in an equation.
- Always make it clear which way the reaction shifts when a condition is altered.
- Include the charge of complex ions in the formula.

Objectives

- To set up an iron(III) complex-ion equilibrium
- To monitor the effect of concentration on the equilibrium
- To know that a dynamic equilibrium exists in a closed system, when the rate of the forward reaction is equal to the rate of the reverse reaction and the concentrations of reactants and products do not change
- To know how Le Châtelier's principle can be used to predict the effect of a change in temperature, pressure or concentration on the position of equilibrium

Equipment

- 0.1 mol dm⁻³ iron(III) chloride, $FeCl_3 \cdot 6H_2O$
- 0.005 mol dm⁻³ potassium thiocyanate, KCNS
- five boiling tubes
- 10 cm³ and 25 cm³ measuring cylinders
- distilled/deionised water

Safety

- Wear eye protection and chemical-resistant gloves.
- Remove strong acids from the working area.
- Iron(III) salts are harmful at this concentration.

Harmful

43

Record your results here.

Analysis of results

- Record your results in an appropriate format.
- Calculate the concentrations of the reagents in each experiment.

....

....

....

....

....

....

....

....

....

- Summarise the shifts in equilibrium with changes in concentration.

....

....

....

....

- Use Le Châtelier's principle to explain your observations.

....

....

....

....

Questions

1 KCNS may be used to test for the presence of Fe^{3+} in solution. From your results, suggest the concentration of KCNS that should be used and how the test should be carried out.

....

....

....

2 The yellow chromate ion, CrO_4^{2-}, changes to the orange dichromate ion, $Cr_2O_7^{2-}$, in the presence of an acid in a reversible reaction. Write a balanced equation for this reaction.

....

....

3 Explain why the addition of alkali, OH^-, causes the orange dichromate ion, $Cr_2O_7^{2-}$, to change back to the yellow chromate ion, CrO_4^{2-}.

....

....

....

....

4 What would you expect to see if some concentrated hydrochloric acid was added to the solution described in question 3?

....

....

....

....

PAG 4

CPAC links		Evidence	Done
1a	Correctly follows instructions to carry out the the experimental techniques or procedures.	Practical observation	
2a	Correctly uses appropriate instrumentation, apparatus and materials (including ICT) to carry out investigative activities, experimental techniques and procedures with minimal assistance or prompting.	Practical observation	
2b	Carries out techniques or procedures methodically, in sequence and in combination, identifying practical issues and making adjustments when necessary.	Method followed	
4b	Obtains accurate, precise and sufficient data for experimental and investigative procedures and records this methodically using appropriate units and conventions.	Results	
5a	Uses appropriate software and/ or tools to process data, carry out research and report findings.	Conclusions	

Objective

- To investigate the effects of temperature on the position of an equilibrium

Equipment

- cobalt chloride hexahydrate
- concentrated hydrochloric acid
- four boiling tubes
- two 250 ml beakers
- ice
- boiling water
- copper(II) chloride
- dropping pipette

Safety

- Wear eye protection and chemical resistant gloves.
- Concentrated hydrochloric acid is corrosive.

Procedure

1   Place half a spatula of cobalt(II) chloride hexahydrate into a boiling tube.

2   Add approximately 4 cm³ of water to the boiling tube. Allow as much of the cobalt chloride hexahydrate to dissolve as possible.

3   Carefully add approximately 6 cm³ of concentrated hydrochloric acid to the boiling tube. Do this by pouring the hydrochloric acid gently down the side of the boiling tube.

4   Thoroughly mix the contents of the boiling tube.

5   Split the contents of the boiling tube approximately equally between two boiling tubes.

6   Stand one of the boiling tubes in an ice bath and leave it for a few minutes. Observe the colour of the mixture.

7   Stand the other boiling tube in a beaker of just boiled water and leave it for a few minutes. Observe the colour of the mixture.

8   Swap the boiling tubes over – place the beaker from the ice bath in the hot water and vice versa. Observe the colours of the mixtures.

9   Add hydrochloric acid dropwise to one of the boiling tubes until there is no further change. Now add water to the same boiling tube until there is no further change.

10 Repeat steps 1 to 9 using copper(II) chloride instead of cobalt chloride hexahydrate.

Learning tips

- Look for patterns in your results.
- Use Le Châtelier's principle to explain any colour changes.

Record your results here.

Record your results for each experiment in a table.

Analysis of results

- The equations for the reactions are:

    $[Co(H_2O)_6]^{2+} + 4Cl^- \rightleftharpoons [CoCl_4]^{2-} + 6H_2O$

    $[Cu(H_2O)_6]^{2+} + 4Cl^- \rightleftharpoons [CuCl_4]^{2-} + 6H_2O$

    Explain the effect of adding water and concentrated hydrochloric acid to each of the reversible reactions.

● What do the results of changing the temperature tell you about each of the reversible reactions? Explain your answer.

....

....

....

....

....

....

....

Questions

1 Indicators are weak acids. They can be represented as HIn. In solution, they exist in the equilibrium:

$HIn \rightleftharpoons H^+ + In^-$

a If dilute sulfuric acid is added to an indicator in solution, what will happen to the position of the equilibrium?

....

....

b Methyl orange is red in hydrochloric acid and yellow in sodium hydroxide solution. What colour is the In^- ion for methyl orange?

....

c At the end point of a titration, methyl orange turns orange. Explain why, in terms of HIn and In^- and their colours.

....

....

....

2 Dichromate(VI) ions and chromate(VI) ions exist in equilibrium.

$Cr_2O_7^{2-} + H_2O \rightleftharpoons 2CrO_4^{2-} + 2H^+$

orange   yellow

Solid sodium chromate is dissolved in water to produce a yellow solution.

a When dilute hydrochloric acid is added to the solution it becomes orange. Explain why.

....

....

....

b If sodium hydroxide is added to the mixture, it becomes yellow again. Explain why.

....

....

....

PAG 5

CPAC links		Evidence	Done
1a	Correctly follows instructions to carry out the experimental techniques or procedures.	Practical observation	
2a	Correctly uses appropriate instrumentation, apparatus and materials (including ICT) to carry out investigative activities, experimental techniques and procedures with minimal assistance or prompting.	Practical observation	
2b	Carries out techniques or procedures methodically, in sequence and in combination, identifying practical issues and making adjustments when necessary.	Method followed	
4b	Obtains accurate, precise and sufficient data for experimental and investigative procedures and records this methodically using appropriate units and conventions.	Results	
5a	Uses appropriate software and/ or tools to process data, carry out research and report findings.	Conclusions and equation	

Diagram

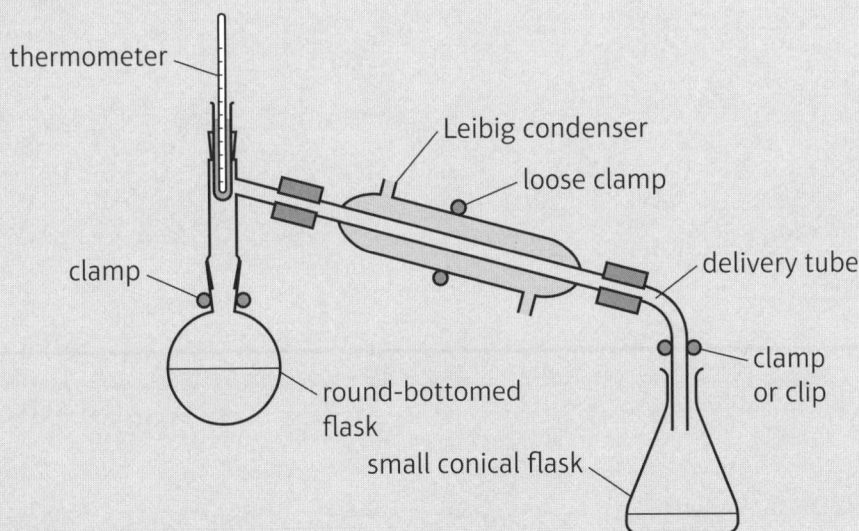

Figure A. Apparatus used to eliminate water from cyclohexanol

Procedure

1   Pour 10 cm³ of cyclohexanol into a boiling tube. Slowly add 4 cm³ of phosphoric(V) acid to the boiling tube. Swirl the flask carefully to ensure complete mixing.

2   Set up the apparatus for distillation as shown in Figure A.

3   Heat the boiling tube in a water bath at 70 °C for 15 minutes.

4   Raise the temperature of the water bath. Distil as slowly as possible so that the vapour is condensed.

Objectives

- To be able to handle glassware
- To know that water can be eliminated from alcohols in the presence of an acid catalyst
- To prove the presence of an alkene using bromine
- To use a separating funnel to remove an organic layer from an aqueous layer and to dry the organic layer using an anhydrous salt

Equipment

- cyclohexanol
- phosphoric(V) acid (H_3PO_4)
- saturated sodium carbonate solution
- anhydrous calcium chloride
- bromine water
- 100 cm³ Quickfit® round-bottomed flask
- Quickfit® dropping funnel
- Quickfit® still head and thermometer pocket
- Quickfit® Liebig condenser
- Quickfit® delivery tube
- water bath at 70 °C
- separating funnel
- two small conical flasks
- mass balance (2 d.p.)
- spatula
- boiling tube and stopper
- two 10 cm³ measuring cylinders

Safety

- Organic compounds are highly flammable, irritant and harmful.
- Wear eye protection.
- Wear chemical-resistant gloves when handling phosphoric(V) acid.
- Bromine water is harmful.

Flammable   Irritant   Harmful

5 Collect the distillate produced between 70 °C and 90 °C.

6 Add an equal volume of saturated sodium carbonate solution to the distillate in a separating funnel.

7 Allow the layers to separate. Discard the lower aqueous layer and run the upper organic layer into a conical flask.

8 Add a few pieces of anhydrous calcium chloride to the top organic layer in the conical flask.

9 Finally, carefully pour the clear liquid into another flask.

10 If you have time, redistill the liquid and collect the distillate produced between 81 °C and 85 °C.

11 Add bromine water dropwise to a few drops of the distillate.

Learning tips

- Understand separation by distillation.
- Appreciate that organic reactions are often slow.
- Make sure you are able to use appropriate purification steps for an organic compound.
- Make sure you are able to write an equation for the reaction that forms cyclohexene.

Record your results here.

Analysis of results
- Record your observations in an appropriate form.
- Write an equation for the reaction.

....

Questions

1 What other chemical would convert cyclohexanol to cyclohexene?

....

....

....

2 Which impurities move into the aqueous layer on shaking with sodium carbonate solution?

....

....

....

....

3 Which impurity is removed by mixing with anhydrous calcium chloride?

....

....

....

....

4 Write an equation for the reaction of cyclohexene with bromine water.

....

....

....

5 How could cyclohexene be produced from bromocyclohexane?

....

....

....

....

PAG 5

CPAC links		Evidence	Done
1a	Correctly follows instructions to carry out the experimental techniques or procedures.	Practical observation	
2a	Correctly uses appropriate instrumentation, apparatus and materials (including ICT) to carry out investigative activities, experimental techniques and procedures with minimal assistance or prompting.	Practical observation	
2b	Carries out techniques or procedures methodically, in sequence and in combination, identifying practical issues and making adjustments when necessary.	Method followed	
4b	Obtains accurate, precise and sufficient data for experimental and investigative procedures and records this methodically using appropriate units and conventions.	Results	
5a	Uses appropriate software and/ or tools to process data, carry out research and report findings.	Conclusions and equation	

Diagram

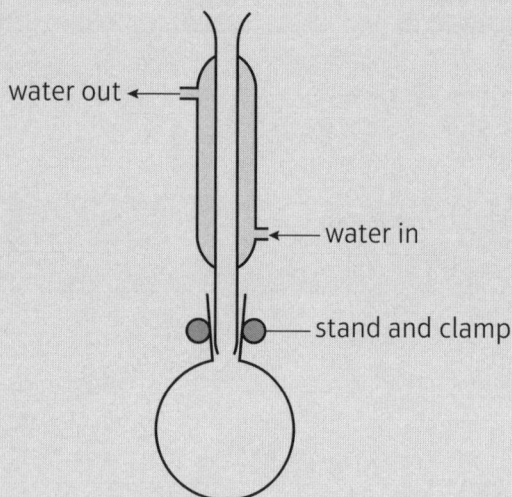

Figure A. Apparatus for reflux

Procedure

1   Slowly add 6 cm³ of concentrated sulfuric acid to 10 cm³ of deionised water in a boiling tube. It will be necessary to cool the tube with iced water as you add the sulfuric acid to the deionised water.

2   Wearing gloves, completely dissolve 10 g of sodium dichromate(VI) in the mixture from step 1 and add a small amount of pumice. *Do not proceed further until all the sodium dichromate has dissolved.*

3   Arrange the apparatus for reflux as shown in Figure A and turn on the water supply to the condenser.

Objectives

- To set up and use *Quickfit®* apparatus for heating under reflux and for distillation
- To separate mixtures by distillation
- To know that primary alcohols can be oxidised by a suitable oxidising agent – such as acidified potassium dichromate – to form aldehydes and carboxylic acids
- To know that the oxidation product can be controlled by using different reaction conditions

Equipment

- ethanol
- concentrated sulfuric acid
- sodium dichromate(VI)
- powdered pumice or small pieces of porcelain
- crushed ice
- deionised/distilled water
- 100 cm³ *Quickfit®* round-bottomed or pear-shaped flask
- *Quickfit®* still head
- *Quickfit®* dropping/separating funnel
- *Quickfit®* Liebig condenser
- *Quickfit®* delivery tube
- conical flask and stopper
- dropping pipette
- beaker
- three 10 cm³ measuring cylinders
- weighing bottle and spatula
- boiling tube and bung
- small Bunsen burner
- mass balance (2 d.p.)
- three stands and clamps

Safety

- Wear eye protection and chemical-resistant gloves.
- Ethanol is flammable.
- Concentrated sulfuric acid is corrosive.
- Sodium dichromate(VI) is a Category 2 carcinogen.

Flammable   Corrosive

4 Mix 3 cm³ of ethanol and 10 cm³ of water in a beaker. Pour this mixture, a little at a time, through the condenser, using iced water to cool the round-bottomed flask as necessary. *Note that this reaction can be very violent and will need frequent cooling.*

5 When all the ethanol solution has been added to the round-bottomed flask, heat it in a water bath and heat under reflux for 30 minutes.

6 Allow the reaction mixture to cool. Now rearrange the apparatus for distillation, as shown in Figure B.

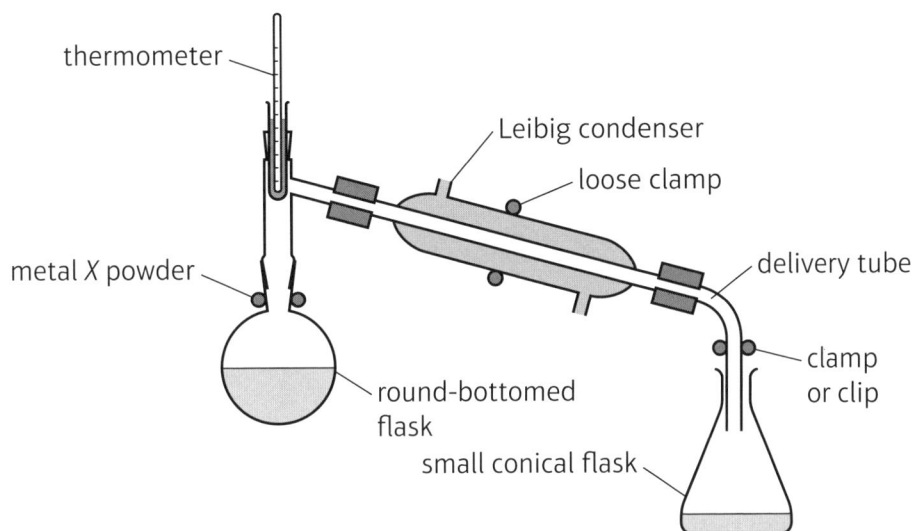

Figure B. Apparatus for distillation

7 Distil using a small blue Bunsen flame and collect approximately 20 cm³ of distillate. The distillate should be aqueous ethanoic acid.

Learning tips

● You should appreciate why reflux, rather than distillation, is used initially in this procedure.

● You should be able to write an equation for this oxidation.

● You should understand why the final distillate is not pure ethanoic acid.

Record your results here.

Analysis of results

● Record your observations in an appropriate form.

● Write an equation for the reaction using [O] to represent the oxidising agent.

....

....

Questions

1 Explain why wine (ethanol) turns to vinegar (ethanoic acid) when it reacts with air.

....

....

....

....

2 Name the acid formed when the ethanol in this reaction is replaced by:

   a propan-1-ol

....

   b pentan-1-ol

....

3 Explain why propan-2-ol is not oxidised to a carboxylic acid.

....

....

....

4 Explain why the distillate may be a mixture of ethanol, ethanal, ethanoic acid and water.

....

....

....

....

....

5 How could the substances mentioned in question 4 be separated?

....

....

....

....

PAG 7

CPAC links		Evidence	Done
1a	Correctly follows instructions to carry out the experimental techniques or procedures.	Practical observation	
2a	Correctly uses appropriate instrumentation, apparatus and materials (including ICT) to carry out investigative activities, experimental techniques and procedures with minimal assistance or prompting.	Practical observation	
2b	Carries out techniques or procedures methodically, in sequence and in combination, identifying practical issues and making adjustments when necessary.	Method followed	
4b	Obtains accurate, precise and sufficient data for experimental and investigative procedures and records this methodically using appropriate units and conventions.	Results	
5a	Uses appropriate software and/or tools to process data, carry out research and report findings.	Analysis	

Objectives

- To carry out hydrolysis reactions
- To know that haloalkanes can be hydrolysed by water in the presence of silver nitrate and ethanol
- To compare the reactivity of haloalkanes experimentally

Equipment

- 1-chlorobutane
- 1-bromobutane
- 1-iodobutane
- ethanol
- silver nitrate solution
- six test tubes, stoppers and labels
- water bath at 50 °C
- stop clock
- 10 cm^3 measuring cylinder
- three dropping pipettes
- hot water
- 0–100 °C thermometer

Safety

- Ethanol and haloalkanes are flammable.
- Wear eye protection.
- Haloalkanes are harmful.

Flammable   Harmful

Procedure

1   Take three test tubes and pour 5 cm^3 of ethanol into each tube. Then add five drops of one of the haloalkanes to each test tube.

2   Put a stopper in each test tube and label the tube. Stand the test tubes in a water bath at 50 °C.

3   Take three clean test tubes and pour 5 cm^3 of silver nitrate solution into each tube. Fit the stoppers and stand the test tubes in the water bath.

4   When all the solutions have reached the temperature of the water bath, add some silver nitrate solution to one of the test tubes containing a haloalkane/ethanol mixture. Start the stop clock as you do so.

5   Time how long it takes for a precipitate to appear.

6   Repeat steps 4 and 5 for the other two haloalkane/ethanol mixtures.

Learning tip

The haloalkane that produces a precipitate first is the most reactive and has the weakest carbon-halogen bond.

Record your results here.

Analysis of results

List the order of reactivity of the haloalkanes.

....

Questions

1   Suggest the order of reactivity for the haloalkanes if the polarity of the C–X bond was the only factor affecting reactivity.

....

2   Suggest the order of reactivity for the haloalkanes if the bond enthalpy of the C–X bond was the only factor affecting reactivity.

....

3   Which of the factors stated in question 1 and question 2 is more important for the reactions seen here?

....

....

4   Explain why using the same number of drops of each haloalkane is not a fair test. Suggest how a fair test could be achieved.

....

....

....

PAG 5

CPAC links		Evidence	Done
1a	Correctly follows instructions to carry out the experimental techniques or procedures.	Practical observation	
2a	Correctly uses appropriate instrumentation, apparatus and materials (including ICT) to carry out investigative activities, experimental techniques and procedures with minimal assistance or prompting.	Practical observation	
2b	Carries out techniques or procedures methodically, in sequence and in combination, identifying practical issues and making adjustments when necessary.	Method followed	
4b	Obtains accurate, precise and sufficient data for experimental and investigative procedures and records this methodically using appropriate units and conventions.	Results	
5a	Uses appropriate software and/ or tools to process data, carry out research and report findings.	Calculations and equation	

Objectives

- To use *Quickfit®* apparatus for distillation and for heating under reflux
- To use a separating funnel to prepare and purify an organic liquid
- To know that haloalkanes can be prepared by substituting a halide ion for a hydroxyl group in the presence of an acid

Equipment

- $10\,cm^3$ measuring cylinder
- $50\,cm^3$ measuring cylinder
- $3.25\,cm^3$ 2-methylpropan-2-ol
- $10\,cm^3$ concentrated hydrochloric acid
- mass balance (2 d.p.)
- $50\,cm^3$ pear-shaped flask
- $50\,cm^3$ separating funnel and stopper
- distillation head
- clamps and stand
- anti-bumping granules
- condenser
- small Bunsen burner or electric heating mantle
- $5\,cm^3$ sodium hydrogencarbonate solution (5%)
- anhydrous sodium sulfate
- two $100\,cm^3$ conical flasks
- 0–110 °C thermometer and holder
- specimen tube
- $50\,cm^3$ beaker

Diagram

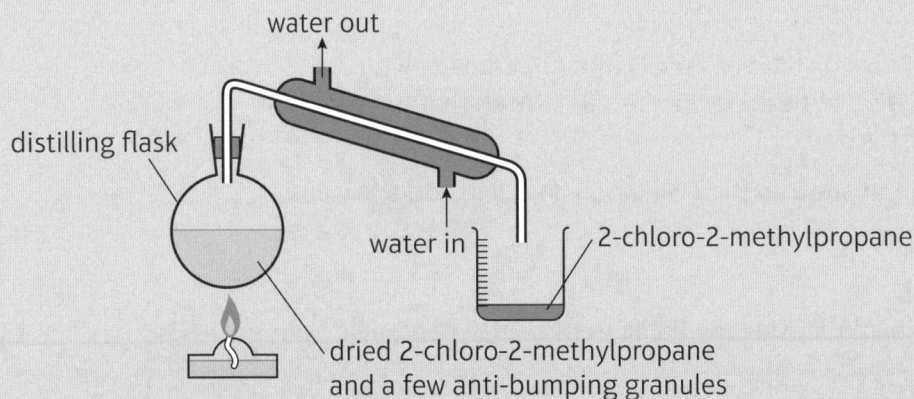

Figure A. Apparatus for simple distillation of 2-chloro-2-methylpropane

Safety

- Concentrated hydrochloric acid is extremely corrosive – avoid skin contact.
- Work in a fume cupboard and avoid inhaling any fumes.
- The vapours produced in this activity can be harmful.
- Wear eye protection and chemical-resistant gloves.
- 2-methylpropan-2-ol is highly flammable and harmful. Keep the bottle stoppered when not in use and keep well away from naked flames. Avoid skin contact and do not breathe in the vapour.

Corrosive   Harmful   Flammable

Procedure

1   Pour approximately 3.25 cm³ of 2-methylpropan-2-ol into a 10 cm³ measuring cylinder. This will be approximately 2.5 g of the 2-methylpropan-2-ol.

2   Weigh the measuring cylinder and its contents and then pour the 2-methylpropan-2-ol into a 50 cm³ separating funnel. Weigh the empty measuring cylinder and record the exact mass of 2-methylpropan-2-ol you have added to the funnel.

3   Pour approximately 10 cm³ of concentrated hydrochloric acid into a 50 cm³ measuring cylinder. Gradually add the acid to the 2-methylpropan-2-ol in the funnel, over a period of approximately 2 minutes.

4   Put the stopper in the funnel and leave the mixture for 20 minutes, shaking it from time to time. After each shake, remove the stopper briefly to release the pressure.

5   Allow the mixture to stand until two layers have separated. Remove the stopper and run the lower layer into a clean 100 cm³ conical flask.

6   Slowly add 5 cm³ of 5% sodium hydrogencarbonate solution to the 2-chloro-2-methylpropane in the separating funnel. Stopper the funnel and shake the contents, gently at first and then more vigorously. There will be a marked build-up of gas, so be very careful when you release the pressure.

7   When the two layers have separated, run off the lower aqueous layer and discard it.

8   Repeat the washing with sodium hydrogencarbonate solution until no more gas is given off.

9   Add 10 cm³ of distilled water to the funnel and shake well.

10 When the two layers have separated, run off and discard the lower aqueous layer. Then run the 2-chloro-2-methylpropane into a clean conical flask.

11 Add small amounts of anhydrous sodium sulfate to the conical flask, swirling after each addition. Anhydrous sodium sulfate acts as a drying agent and removes the last traces of water. Add the drying agent until the liquid is totally clear.

12 Set up clean and dry apparatus for simple distillation (see Figure A), complete with thermometer. The thermometer bulb should be opposite the side-arm so that it measures the temperature of the liquid that distils over.

13 Transfer the dried 2-chloro-2-methylpropane into the distillation flask and add a few anti-bumping granules.

14 Weigh a clean, dry specimen tube.

15 Gently heat the liquid in the distillation flask using the flame from a small hand-held Bunsen burner.

16 At first, use a small beaker as the receiver. Start collecting the 2-chloro-2-methylpropane in the weighed specimen tube when the temperature reaches 48 °C. The boiling point of 2-chloro-2-methylpropane is 51 °C.

17 Stop the distillation when the temperature recorded by the thermometer rises above 53 °C. Put the stopper in the specimen tube and record the mass of 2-chloro-2-methylpropane collected.

Learning tip

The preparation of an organic compound usually covers four stages:

●   carrying out the reaction

●   separating the required product from the reaction mixture

●   purifying the product

●   testing the product to check that it is a pure sample of the required compound.

Record your results here.

Analysis of results

- Write an equation for the reaction you have carried out.

  ....

- Use the mass of 2-methylpropan-2-ol that you started with (or assume it was 2.5 g) to calculate the expected yield of 2-chloro-2-methylpropane.

  ....

  ....

- Use the yield of 2-chloro-2-methylpropane you actually produced to calculate the percentage yield of the compound.

  ....

  ....

- Comment on the yield of this reaction.

  ....

  ....

Questions

1   What impurities are likely to be contaminating the 2-chloro-2-methylpropane layer in stage 4?

    ....

    ....

2   Which impurity is removed by shaking the product with a solution of sodium hydrogencarbonate?

    ....

3   Why is there a marked build-up of pressure during the shaking?

    ....

    ....

4   Suggest a reason why sodium hydrogencarbonate solution is used rather than sodium hydroxide solution.

    ....

    ....

5   How does the final stage act as a check for the identity and the purity of the product?

    ....

    ....

    ....

6   Suggest three reasons why the yield of your experiment was so low.

    ....

    ....

    ....

PAG 8

CPAC links		Evidence	Done
1a	Correctly follows instructions to carry out the experimental techniques or procedures.	Practical procedure	
2a	Correctly uses appropriate instrumentation, apparatus and materials (including ICT) to carry out investigative activities, experimental techniques and procedures with minimal assistance or prompting.	Practical procedure	
4b	Obtains accurate, precise and sufficient data for experimental and investigative procedures and records this methodically using appropriate units and conventions.	Measurements and results table	

Objectives

- To construct an electrochemical cell
- To measure the cell potential of a selection of electrochemical cells

Equipment

- 50 cm³ of 0.4 mol dm⁻³ zinc sulfate solution
- 50 cm³ of 0.4 mol dm⁻³ copper(II) sulfate solution
- 50 cm³ of 1 mol dm⁻³ iron(II) sulfate solution
- 50 cm³ of 0.1 mol dm⁻³ silver nitrate solution
- saturated potassium nitrate solution
- distilled/deionised water
- one strip of each of zinc, copper, iron and silver
- sandpaper
- four 100 cm³ beakers
- strips of filter paper about 12 cm long
- 100 cm³ measuring cylinder
- voltmeter (20 V) reading to 2 d.p.
- connecting wires and crocodile clips

Diagram

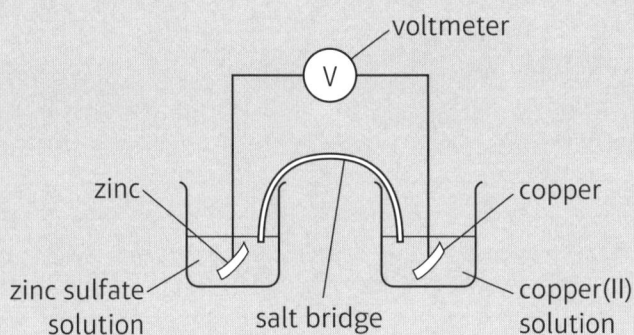

Safety

- Wear eye protection and disposable nitrile gloves.
- Zinc sulfate is harmful.
- 1 mol dm⁻³ iron(II) sulfate is harmful.
- Potassium nitrate is oxidising.

Procedure

1 Clean the strips of zinc and copper using sandpaper.

2 Set up a zinc half-cell by pouring 50 cm³ of zinc sulfate solution into a 100 cm³ beaker and standing the strip of zinc in the beaker.

3 Set up a copper half-cell by pouring 50 cm³ of copper(II) sulfate solution into a separate 100 cm³ beaker and standing the strip of copper in the beaker.

4 Make an electrical connection between the two beakers by joining them with a strip of filter paper that has been dipped in a saturated solution of potassium nitrate, as shown in the diagram. This is known as a salt bridge.

5 Join the two metal strips with a voltmeter, using the connecting wires and crocodile clips.

6 Record the cell potential of the [Zn(s) | Zn²⁺(aq)] and [Cu²⁺(aq) | Cu(s)] system. If the voltmeter gives a negative value, reverse the connections so that it gives a positive value.

7 Now, repeat steps 1–6 using the following combinations of metal/metal ion half-cells. Remember to clean the metal strips with sandpaper before use.
[Zn(s) | Zn²⁺(aq)] and [Fe²⁺(aq) | Fe(s)]
[Fe(s) | Fe²⁺(aq)] and [Cu²⁺(aq) | Cu(s)]
[Zn(s) | Zn²⁺(aq)] and [Ag⁺(aq) | Ag(s)]
[Cu(s) | Cu²⁺(aq)] and [Ag⁺(aq) | Ag(s)]

8 Prepare a suitable results table to record the cell potential for each of the five cells you have set up. Record your results to an appropriate precision.

Learning tip

Note that the concentration of silver nitrate used is 0.1 mol dm^{-3}, which is different to the other solutions. It is particularly dangerous to handle 1 mol dm^{-3} silver nitrate. The reference data below shows the results for 1 mol dm^{-3} silver nitrate for you to compare.

Record your results here.

Analysis of results

- A standard electrode potential of one of the half-cells can be calculated by combining the cell potential and the electrode potential of the other half-cell.

- To calculate $E^{\ominus}$ [Zn^{2+}(aq) | Zn(s)], substitute the values given into the equation:

$E^{\ominus}_{cell} = E^{\ominus}_{\text{right-hand half-cell}} - E^{\ominus}_{\text{left-hand half-cell}}$

For example, assume that in the first cell you set up, the [Zn(s) | Zn^{2+}(aq)] and [Cu^{2+}(aq) | Cu(s)] system:

$E^{\ominus}_{cell}$ = 1.10 V

$E^{\ominus}$ [Cu^{2+}(aq) | Cu(s)] = +0.34 V

Use these values and the equation above to calculate $E^{\ominus}$ [Zn^{2+}(aq) | Zn(s)].

....

....

Reference data

Standard cell potentials for these cells are:

[Zn(s) | Zn^{2+}(aq)] and [Cu^{2+}(aq) | Cu(s)] = 1.10 V

[Zn(s) | Zn^{2+}(aq)] and [Fe^{2+}(aq) | Fe(s)] = 0.32 V

[Fe(s) | Fe^{2+}(aq)] and [Cu^{2+}(aq) | Cu(s)] = 0.78 V

[Zn(s) | Zn^{2+}(aq)] and [A^{+}(aq) | Ag(s)] = 1.56 V*

[Cu(s) | Cu^{2+}(aq)] and [Ag^{+}(aq) | Ag(s)] = 0.46 V*

*Assumes the solution of silver ions is 1.0 mol dm^{-3}

Questions

1 Using your results and the value $E^{\ominus}$ [Cu^{2+}(aq) | Cu(s)] = +0.34 V, calculate $E^{\ominus}$ [Fe^{2+}(aq) | Fe(s)].

....

....

....

....

....

....

....

2 The observed cell potential values for the cells that you set up may be slightly different to theoretical values. Give a reason for this.

....

....

....

....

....

....

3 Give a reason why silver nitrate is not used as a 1 mol dm^{-3} solution.

....

....

....

....

....

4 Mg^{2+}(aq)/Mg(s) can also be used as a half-cell. Describe a problem that might be observed with this system.

....

....

....

....

....

....

PAG 1

CPAC links		Evidence	Done
1a	Correctly follows instructions to carry out the experimental techniques or procedures.	Practical procedure	
2a	Correctly uses appropriate instrumentation, apparatus and materials (including ICT) to carry out investigative activities, experimental techniques and procedures with minimal assistance or prompting.	Practical procedure	
4b	Obtains accurate, precise and sufficient data for experimental and investigative procedures and records this methodically using appropriate units and conventions.	Measurements and results table	

Procedure

1   Crush the iron tablets using the pestle and mortar.

2   Transfer the crushed tablets to a weighing boat and measure their combined mass. Record this mass in the space below.

3   Empty the crushed tablets into the small beaker and re-weigh the weighing boat. Record this mass in the space below.

4   Add 100 cm³ 1.5 mol dm⁻³ of sulfuric acid to the small beaker. Stir to dissolve as much of the tablets as possible.

5   Filter the solution (to remove any undissolved solids) into the volumetric flask. Rinse the beaker with more sulfuric acid and add the washings to the volumetric flask. Make up to the mark with distilled/deionised water. Stopper and shake.

6   Pipette 25 cm³ of this solution into the conical flask.

7   Titrate the iron(II) solution with potassium manganate(VII) solution until the mixture has just turned pink. On standing, the pink colour will disappear because there is a secondary reaction between the $KMnO_4$ and another ingredient in the tablet. Do not add any more $KMnO_4$.

8   Record your results in an appropriate format in the space below.

9   Repeat the titration until concordant results are obtained.

Learning tips

- You need to use two equations:

$$moles = concentration \times \frac{volume}{1000}$$

$$moles = \frac{mass}{M_r}$$

- Show all working carefully in a titration calculation and explain what you are doing in each step.
  That way you can still gain marks in an exam, even if you get the final answer wrong.

Objectives

- To calculate the percentage of iron in an iron tablet
- To perform a redox titration involving $Fe^{2+}(aq)$ and $MnO_4^-(aq)$

Equipment

- eye protection
- labels, OHP pen or grease pencil
- glucose dilutions: 10%, 1%, 0.1%, 0.01%
- distilled water
- unknown glucose solution
- Benedict's solution
- three 1 cm³ syringes
- six boiling tubes
- boiling tube tongs
- kettle or a pre-set water bath
- 500 cm³ beaker
- 250 cm³ water
- five iron tablets
- 100 cm³ of 1.5 mol dm⁻³ sulfuric acid
- 100 cm³ of 0.005 mol dm⁻³ potassium manganate(VII)
- distilled/deionised water
- pestle and mortar
- 100 cm³ beaker
- 25 cm³ measuring cylinder
- two 250 cm³ beakers
- 250 cm³ volumetric flask, stoppered
- spatula, glass rod and dropping pipettes
- filter funnel and filter paper
- 50 cm³ burette and burette stand
- 25 cm³ pipette and pipette filler
- 250 cm³ conical flask
- white tile
- mass balance (2 d.p.) and weighing boat

Record your results here.

Use your concordant results to calculate the average titre and then answer the questions below to calculate the mass of iron in one tablet.

Average titre = ...

Questions

1   Combine the two half-equations given below to write the equation for the reaction:

$$Fe^{2+}(aq) \rightarrow Fe^{3+} + e^-$$

$$MnO_4^-(aq) + 8H^+(aq) + 5e^- \rightarrow Mn^{2+}(aq) + 4H_2O(l)$$

M_r Fe = 55.8

....

....

2   Use your average titre to calculate the number of moles of manganate(VII) ions that were used in the titration.

....

....

....

....

3   Use the equation to calculate the number of moles of iron(II) ions in the 25 cm³ sample of iron(II) sulfate from the iron tablet.

....

....

4 Calculate the number of moles of iron(II) ions in the 250 cm³ graduated flask at the start of the experiment.

....

....

....

....

....

5 Calculate the mass of Fe in the original five iron tablets, and hence the mass of Fe in one iron tablet.

....

....

....

....

....

6 Compare your value for the mass of Fe with the information from the supplier about the composition of each iron tablet.

....

....

7 Evaluate the procedure and make a list of any sources of procedural errors. Suggest ways in which these errors can be avoided.

....

....

....

....

....

....

....

....

8 Calculate the percentage measurement uncertainty in the average titre.

....

....

....

PAG 10

CPAC links		Evidence	Done
1a	Correctly follows instructions to carry out the experimental techniques or procedures.	Practical procedure	
2a	Correctly uses appropriate instrumentation, apparatus and materials (including ICT) to carry out investigative activities, experimental techniques and procedures with minimal assistance or prompting.	Practical procedure	
4b	Obtains accurate, precise and sufficient data for experimental and investigative procedures and records this methodically using appropriate units and conventions.	Measurements and results table	

Objectives

- To use a clock reaction to find the order of reaction with respect to iodide ions
- To use a clock reaction to find the order of reaction with respect to persulfate ions

Equipment

- $100\,cm^3$ of $0.2\,mol\,dm^{-3}$ sodium persulfate solution
- $100\,cm^3$ of $0.2\,mol\,dm^{-3}$ potassium iodide solution
- $50\,cm^3$ of $0.05\,mol\,dm^{-3}$ sodium thiosulfate solution
- $20\,cm^3$ of 1% starch solution
- distilled/deionised water
- white tile
- four $10\,cm^3$ measuring cylinders
- dropping pipettes
- four $100\,cm^3$ beakers
- four $250\,cm^3$ beakers
- stop clock

Safety ⚠

- Wear a lab coat and eye protection.
- Tie long hair back.

Procedure

1 Measure out $10\,cm^3$ of $0.2\,mol\,dm^{-3}$ potassium iodide solution into a small beaker standing on a white tile.

2 Add $5\,cm^3$ of $0.05\,mol\,dm^{-3}$ sodium thiosulfate solution to the potassium iodide solution.

3 Add 10 drops of starch solution to the mixture in the small beaker. The starch is acting as the indicator and must be used in each experiment.

4 Measure out $10\,cm^3$ of the $0.2\,mol\,dm^{-3}$ sodium persulfate solution. Pour this into the mixture prepared in steps 1 and 2. Start the stop clock.

5 Stop the stop clock when a blue colour appears in the beaker. Note the time taken for this to occur.

6 Record your results in Table 2.

7 Repeat steps 1–5 using the volumes of sodium persulfate and potassium iodide solutions shown in Table 1. Note the total volume, including the sodium thiosulfate solution, must always add up to $25\,cm^3$, which can be achieved by adding the correct volume of deionised water.

Table 1

Mixture	Vol. $S_2O_8^{2-}$/cm³	Vol. I^-/cm³	Vol. $S_2O_3^{2-}$/cm³	Vol. H_2O/cm³
A	10	10	5	0
B	10	8	5	2
C	10	6	5	4
D	10	4	5	6
E	10	2	5	8
F	8	10	5	2
G	6	10	5	4
H	4	10	5	6
I	2	10	5	8

Learning tips

- The initial rate is the instantaneous rate at the start of a reaction, when the time $t = 0$. The initial rate can be found by measuring the gradient of a tangent drawn at $t = 0$ on a concentration–time graph.

- A clock reaction is a more convenient way of obtaining the initial rate of a reaction by taking a single measurement. The time, t, from the start of an experiment for a visual change to be observed is measured. This often involves a colour change or the formation of a precipitate.

- If there is no significant change in rate during this time, it can be assumed that the average rate of reaction will be the same as the initial rate. The initial rate is then proportional to $\frac{1}{t}$.

Determining order from a rate–concentration graph

Zero order with respect to A $1/t(\propto \text{rate}) = k[A]^0$	First order with respect to A $1/t(\propto \text{rate}) = k[A]^1$	Second order with respect to A $1/t(\propto \text{rate}) = k[A]^2$
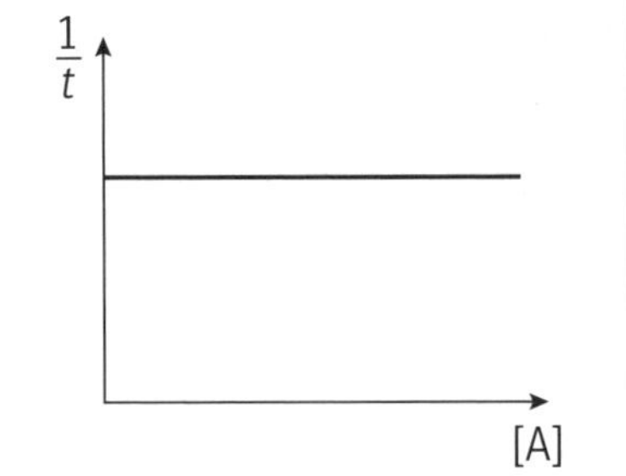	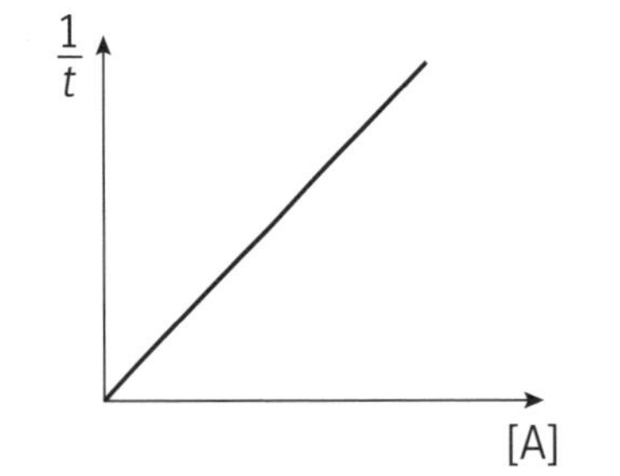	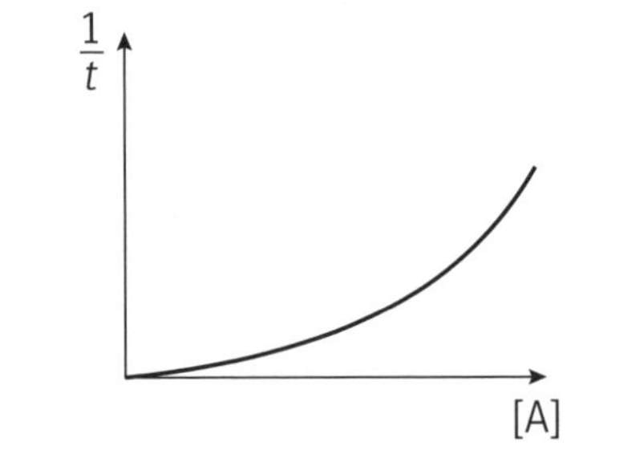

It is impossible to determine directly by sight from a rate–concentration graph that the reaction is second order. If the graph is a curve as shown on the right, then it is necessary to plot $\frac{1}{t}$ against $[A]^2$. If this produces a straight line passing through the origin, then the reaction is second order with respect to A.

Record your results here.

Table 2

Mixture	Conc. $S_2O_8^{2-}$/mol dm^{-3}	Conc. I$^-$/mol dm^{-3}	Time, t/s	$1/t$ ($\propto$ rate) /s^{-1}
A				
B				
C				
D				
E				
F				
G				
H				
I				

Analysis of results

- Calculate the concentration of iodide ions in each of the 25 cm³ solutions for experiments A–E. Write these values in Table 2.

....

....

....

....

....

....

....

....

....

- Use the times recorded in each experiment to work out the rates for these experiments. Write these values in Table 2.

....

....

....

....

....

....

....

- Plot a graph of rate against concentration. Deduce the order of the reaction with respect to iodide ions.

....

....

....

....

....

....

....

Plot your graph here.

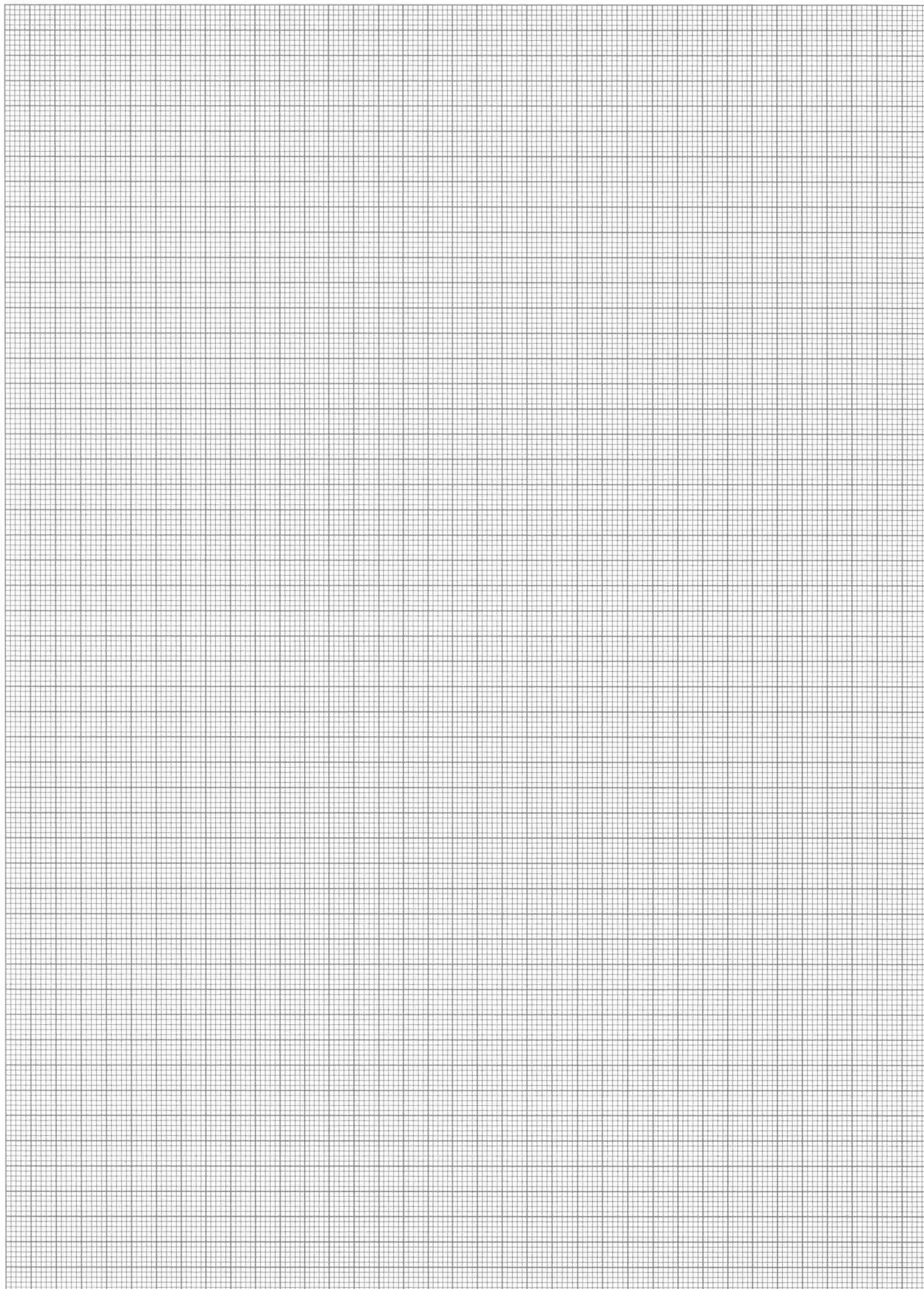

- Using the data from mixture A and that from mixtures F–I, work out the concentration of the persulfate ions in 25 cm³ of solution.
  Write these values in Table 2.

....
....
....
....
....
....
....
....
....

- Work out the rate for each of these concentrations.
  Write these values in Table 2.

....
....
....
....
....
....
....

- Plot a graph of rate against concentration. Deduce the order of the reaction with respect to persulfate ions.

....
....
....
....
....
....

Plot your graph here.

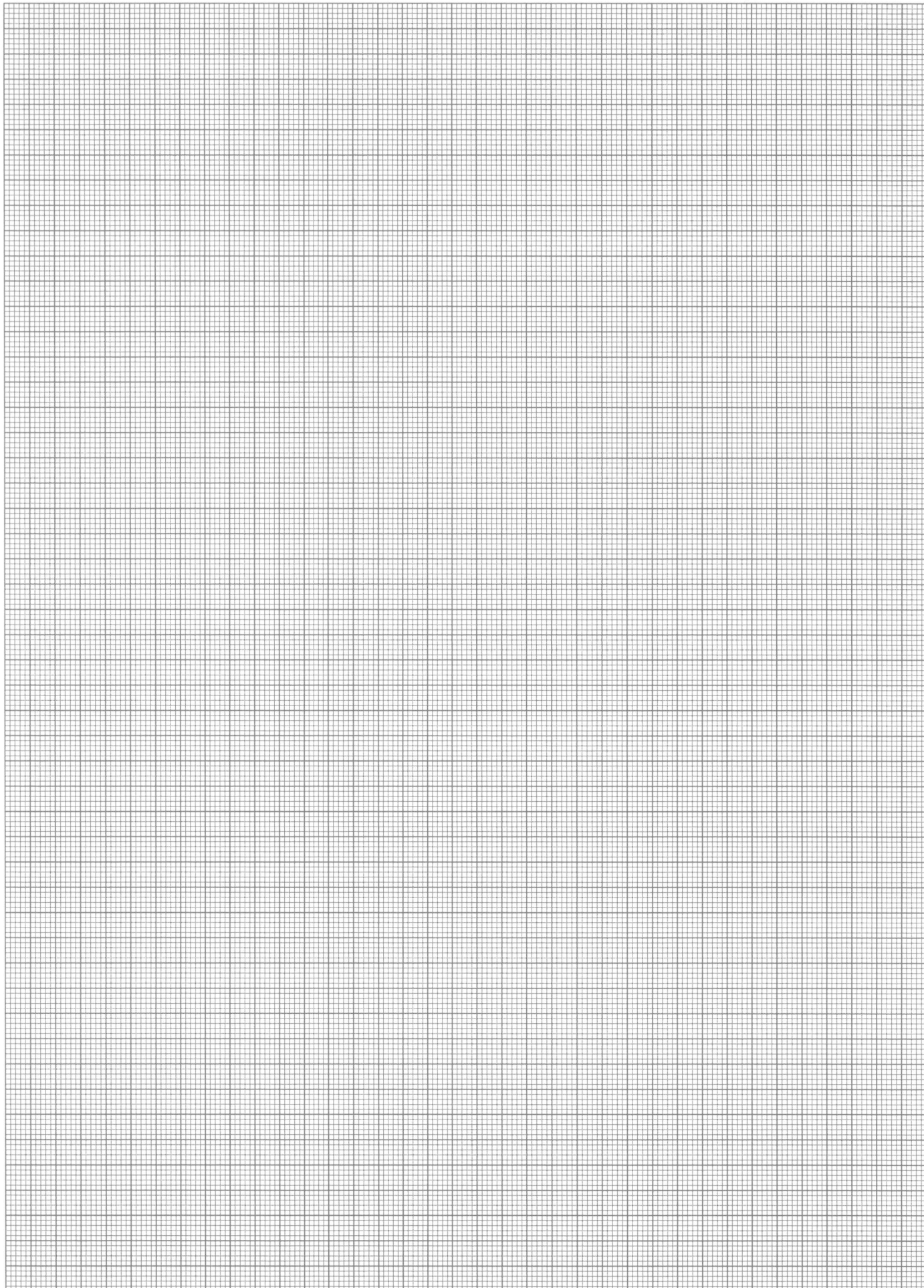

Questions

1 Identify the main sources of error in the procedure used and uncertainties in the measurements recorded in this experiment. Calculate the percentage error for any measurements taken.

....

....

....

....

....

....

....

....

....

....

....

....

2 Suggest ways of minimising these errors.

....

....

....

....

....

3 What is the overall rate equation for this reaction?

....

....

4 The equation for this reaction is:

$S_2O_8^{2-} + 2I^- \rightarrow 2SO_4^{2-} + I_2$

A suggested mechanism for the reaction is:

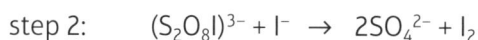

step 1: $I^- + S_2O_8^{2-} \rightarrow (S_2O_8I)^{3-}$

step 2: $(S_2O_8I)^{3-} + I^- \rightarrow 2SO_4^{2-} + I_2$

Which of these steps is the rate-determining step? Use the rate equation to justify your answer.

....

....

....

....

PAG 6

CPAC links		Evidence	Done
1a	Correctly follows instructions to carry out the experimental techniques or procedures.	Practical procedure	
2a	Correctly uses appropriate instrumentation, apparatus and materials (including ICT) to carry out investigative activities, experimental techniques and procedures with minimal assistance or prompting.	Practical procedure	
2b	Carries out techniques or procedures methodically, in sequence and in combination, identifying practical issues and making adjustments when necessary.	Practical procedure and answers to questions	
3b	Uses appropriate safety equipment and approaches to minimise risks with minimal prompting.	Practical procedure	
4b	Obtains accurate, precise and sufficient data for experimental and investigative procedures and records this methodically using appropriate units and conventions.	Measurements and results table	

Objectives

- To perform and explain the reactions of acid anhydrides
- To synthesise aspirin from 2-hydroxybenzoic acid

Equipment

- $10\ cm^3$ of ethanoic anhydride
- 2 g of 2-hydroxybenzoic acid
- $1\ cm^3$ of concentrated sulfuric acid
- distilled/deionised water
- two $10\ cm^3$ measuring cylinders
- condenser
- pear-shaped flask
- stand, clamp and boss
- two $250\ cm^3$ beakers
- dropping pipettes
- ice
- Bunsen burner, tripod, gauze and safety mat
- mass balance (2 d.p.) and weighing boats
- Büchner funnel, Büchner flask, water/suction pump and filter paper to fit funnel
- melting point apparatus and melting point tubes

Safety

- Perform the experiment in a well-ventilated room.
- Wear a lab coat and eye protection.
- Wear heat-protective gloves when handling hot equipment.
- Tie long hair back.
- Ethanoic anhydride is corrosive.
- Concentrated sulfuric acid is corrosive.
- 2-hydroxybenzoic acid is harmful.

Diagram

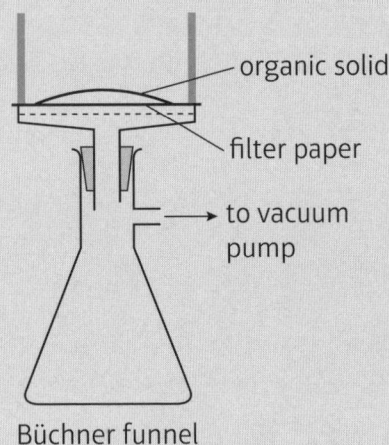

Figure A. Using a Büchner funnel for filtration under reduced pressure

Procedure

1 Weigh 2 g of 2-hydroxybenzoic acid and put it in a pear-shaped flask. Record the mass in the space provided. Clamp the flask and suspend it in a beaker of water.

2 Add $5\ cm^3$ of ethanoic anhydride to the 2-hydroxybenzoic acid. Add five drops of concentrated sulfuric acid to the mixture in the flask. Fix a condenser on the flask.

3 In a fume cupboard, carefully warm the mixture in the water bath using a Bunsen burner. Gently swirl the mixture until all the solid has dissolved.

4   Continue warming the mixture for another 10 minutes.

5   Remove the flask from the hot water bath and add 10 cm³ of crushed ice and some distilled/deionised water to break down any unreacted ethanoic anhydride.

6   Stand the flask in a beaker of iced water until precipitation appears to be complete.

7   Filter off the product using a Büchner funnel and suction apparatus.

8   Wash the crystals with the minimum volume of iced water.

9   Recrystallise the aspirin in the minimum volume of a mixture of ethanol to water (1 : 3).

10   Filter and dry.

11   Measure the mass of the pure, dry crystals. Record the mass in the space below.

12   Measure and record the melting point of the product using melting point apparatus.

Learning tip

$$\text{Percentage yield} = \frac{\text{actual yield}}{\text{expected yield}} \times 100$$

Record your results here.

Analysis of results

Record the mass of dry aspirin obtained and its melting point range.

....

....

....

....

....

....

Questions

1 Which functional group of the 2-hydroxybenzoic acid reacts with the ethanoic anhydride?

....

2 Draw the structural formulae for the reactants and product involved in the formation of aspirin from 2-hydroxybenzoic acid.

3 Calculate the relative molecular masses of 2-hydroxybenzoic acid and aspirin.

....

....

....

....

....

4 Calculate the theoretical yield of aspirin from your experiment.

....

....

Questions

....

....

5 Calculate the percentage yield of aspirin from your experiment.

....

....

....

....

6 Why might the apparent yield be higher?

....

....

....

7 Comment on the reasons for the losses that have occurred during the preparation and the purification of the solid.

....

....

....

....

....

....

8 Give two advantages of filtering under reduced pressure.

....

....

9 What would you expect to be the main impurity in your sample?

....

....

10 The actual melting point of aspirin is 136 °C. Is this similar to the value you recorded? Why do you think there might have been a difference?

....

....

....

....

....

....

PAG 3

CPAC links		Evidence	Done
1a	Correctly follows instructions to carry out the experimental techniques or procedures.	Practical procedure	
2a	Correctly uses appropriate instrumentation, apparatus and materials (including ICT) to carry out investigative activities, experimental techniques and procedures with minimal assistance or prompting.	Practical procedure	
2b	Carries out techniques or procedures methodically, in sequence and in combination, identifying practical issues and making adjustments when necessary.	Practical procedure and answers to questions	
2d	Selects appropriate equipment and measurement strategies in order to ensure suitably accurate results.	Practical procedure	
4b	Obtains accurate, precise and sufficient data for experimental and investigative procedures and records this methodically using appropriate units and conventions.	Measurements and results table	

Objectives

- To calculate an enthalpy change of solution
- To compare enthalpy changes of solution for the chlorides of Group 1

Equipment

- 10 g of lithium chloride
- 10 g of sodium chloride
- 10 g of potassium chloride
- distilled/deionised water
- 100 cm³ measuring cylinder
- polystyrene cup and lid
- thermometer (−10 – 110 °C)
- mass balance (2 d.p.) and weighing boats
- spatula

Safety

- Wear eye protection.
- Lithium chloride is harmful.

Diagram

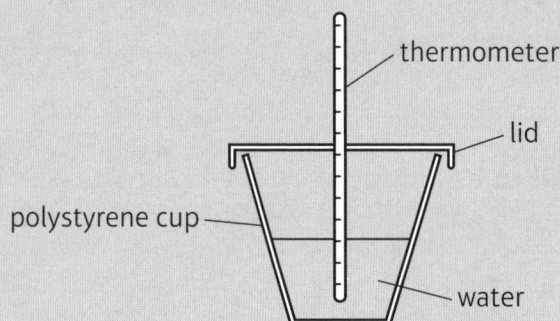

Procedure

1 Measure 50 cm³ of water using a measuring cylinder and pour it into the polystyrene cup.

2 Fix the lid on the cup and stand the cup in a beaker to keep it stable. Measure the temperature of the water (see diagram). Record the temperature in the space provided.

3 The mass of 0.1 moles of lithium chloride is 4.24 g. Weigh that amount of lithium chloride into a weighing boat.

4 Remove the lid from the polystyrene cup and add the lithium chloride. Quickly replace the lid and stir the solution steadily using the thermometer. Record the highest and lowest temperatures as the salt dissolves.

5 Repeat this procedure using sodium chloride and then potassium chloride. You will need to calculate the mass of 0.1 moles of each substance. The M_r values you need are: Na = 23.0, Cl = 35.5 and K = 39.1.

Learning tip

Use the equation $q = mc\Delta T$ to calculate the energy transferred to the water.

Record your results here.

Analysis of results

Calculate the energy transferred to the water for each solution.

....

....

....

....

....

....

Sample data

Temperature changes of:

13.5 °C for LiCl

−2.0 °C for NaCl

−8.0 °C for KCl

Specific heat capacity of water = $4.18 \, J \, g^{-1} \, K^{-1}$

Lattice enthalpy of LiCl = $-849 \, kJ \, mol^{-1}$

Enthalpy of hydration of $Cl^-(g)$ = $-384.1 \, kJ \, mol^{-1}$

Questions

1 Calculate the enthalpy change of solution for each of the three chlorides.

....

....

....

....

....

....

....

....

2 Describe and explain the trend in the enthalpy changes of solution for the Group 1 chlorides.

....

....

....

....

....

....

....

....

3 Predict the enthalpy change of solution for caesium chloride.

....

....

4 Use the data from your experiments and the sample data given to work out the enthalpy of hydration of the lithium ion, Li^+.

   lattice enthalpy + enthalpy change of solution = enthalpy of hydration of $Li^+(g)$ + enthalpy of hydration of $Cl^-(g)$.

....

....

....

....

5 Evaluate the procedure and make a list of sources of procedural and measurement errors in this experiment.

....

....

....

....

....

....

....

....

....

....

....

....

....

....

....

....

6 Give ways in which these procedural and measurement errors could be overcome.

....

....

....

....

....

....

....

....

....

....

....

....

PAG **4**

CPAC links		Evidence	Done
1a	Correctly follows instructions to carry out the experimental techniques or procedures.	Practical procedure	
3b	Uses appropriate safety equipment and approaches to minimise risks with minimal prompting.	Practical procedure	
4a	Makes accurate observations relevant to the experimental or investigative procedure.	Results table	

Procedure

Teacher demonstration

1   Pour 1 cm^3 of the cobalt(II) nitrate solution into a test tube. Add concentrated hydrochloric acid drop-wise to the cobalt solution until there are no further changes.

Student practical

1   Record the colour of each of these solutions *before* and *after* the addition of each reagent.

2   Pour 0.5 cm^3 of copper(II) sulfate solution into a test tube. Add concentrated hydrochloric acid drop-wise to the copper solution until there are no further changes. *Keep this solution*.

3   Put 0.5 cm^3 of copper(II) sulfate solution into a test tube. Add concentrated ammonia solution drop-wise to the copper solution until there are no further changes.

4   Take the solution from Step 2 and add concentrated ammonia solution drop-wise to the copper solution until there are no further changes.

Learning tip

A colour change indicates that there has been a change of ligand. Look at what solutions you have mixed to work out the formula of the complex ion formed.

Objectives

- To perform reactions involving the replacement of ligands
- To relate ligand substitution of complexes to the stability constant

Equipment

- 1 cm^3 of 0.5 mol dm^{-3} solution of copper(II) sulfate
- 1 cm^3 of 0.5 mol dm^{-3} solution of cobalt(II) nitrate
- concentrated hydrochloric acid solution
- concentrated ammonia solution
- three test tubes
- one test tube rack
- graduated dropping pipettes or 10 cm^3 measuring cylinders

Safety

- Wear eye protection.
- Copper(II) sulfate is low hazard and not dangerous to the environment.
- Cobalt(II) nitrate is toxic and dangerous to the environment – it should only be handled by the teacher or technician.
- Concentrated hydrochloric acid solution is corrosive and should be kept in the fume cupboard.
- Concentrated ammonia solution is corrosive and dangerous to the environment. Keep in the fume cupboard. Keep away from the hydrochloric acid solution.

Record the colour changes here.

Conclusion

Write a conclusion to discuss your results.

....

....

....

....

....

....

....

Questions

1   Which ligand is replacing the water in Step 2? Write an equation for this process.

   ....

   ....

   ....

2   Which ligand is replacing the water in Step 3? Write an equation for this process.

   ....

   ....

   ....

3   Which ligand is replacing the water in the teacher demonstration? Write an equation for this process.

   ....

   ....

   ....

4   Name the ligand bonding with the copper(II) ion in Step 4 and state what it has been replaced by.
   Give an equation for the reaction.

   ....

   ....

   ....

5   Place the complex ions formed between the copper(II) ion and ammonia, the copper(II) ion and chloride ions and
   the copper(II) ion and water in order of increasing stability. Explain why you have put them in this order.

   ....

   ....

   ....

   ....

   ....

6   The stability constants for the formation of the copper(II)/ammonia complex and the copper(II)/chloride complex
   are approximately 10^{13} and 10^6, respectively. Does this confirm the order of stability you have given in your
   answer to Question 5? Explain why.

   ....

   ....

   ....

   ....

PAG 7

CPAC links		Evidence	Done
1a	Correctly follows instructions to carry out the experimental techniques or procedures.	Practical procedure	
2a	Correctly uses appropriate instrumentation, apparatus and materials (including ICT) to carry out investigative activities, experimental techniques and procedures with minimal assistance or prompting.	Practical procedure	
2b	Carries out techniques or procedures methodically, in sequence and in combination, identifying practical issues and making adjustments when necessary.	Practical procedure	
3b	Uses appropriate safety equipment and approaches to minimise risks with minimal prompting.	Practical procedure	
4a	Makes accurate observations relevant to the experimental or investigative procedure.	Results table	

Procedure

1 Dissolve five drops of propanal in 0.5 cm^3 of methanol. Add 3 cm^3 of 2,4-dinitrophenylhydrazine (2,4-DNPH) solution.

2 Stopper the test tube and mix the solution by rocking it from side to side. Record your observations.

3 Repeat steps 1 and 2 using propanone instead of propanal.

4 Now identify one of the unknown carbonyl compounds (X, Y or Z). Pour 0.5 cm^3 of methanol into a test tube and add 10 drops of one of the unknown aldehydes or ketones. If the unknown compound does not dissolve, add more methanol drop-by-drop.

5 Add 5 cm^3 of 2,4-DNPH to this solution. Stopper the test tube and shake it. If a precipitate does not form readily, add a few drops of dilute sulfuric acid until a precipitate appears.

6 Filter the precipitate under reduced pressure using a small Büchner funnel. Wash with the minimum volume of cold methanol.

7 Recrystallise the precipitate using a solvent of ethanol and water (mixed in equal volumes). Warm the solvent using hot water and dissolve the crystals in the minimum volume of solvent.

8 Remove any undissolved solids by filtering the solution using an ordinary filter funnel and filter paper while hot, and then allow the filtrate to cool to room temperature. Crystals should form as the filtrate cools.

9 Filter the pure crystals under reduced pressure using a Büchner funnel and flask. Dry at room temperature.

10 Measure and record the melting point of the pure, dry product using melting point apparatus.

Objectives

- To perform the characteristic test for a carbonyl compound
- To use the techniques of recrystallisation and melting point determination to identify an unknown carbonyl compound

Equipment

- 2 cm^3 of methanol
- 12 cm^3 of 2,4-dinitrophenylhydrazine (2,4-DNPH)
- propanal
- propanone
- carbonyl compound X
- carbonyl compound Y
- carbonyl compound Z
- 0.5 mol dm^{-3} sulfuric acid solution
- 10 cm^3 of ethanol
- graduated dropping pipette
- four dropping pipettes
- two 10 cm^3 measuring cylinders
- four test tubes and stoppers
- filter funnel, filter paper and 100 cm^3 conical flask
- Büchner funnel, Büchner flask with water (suction) pump and filter paper to fit funnel
- melting point apparatus and melting point tubes
- kettle

Safety

- Wear eye protection and disposable nitrile gloves.
- Carbonyl compounds, propanal, propanone, methanol and ethanol are all flammable.
- Methanol and 2,4-dinitrophenylhydrazine are toxic.
- Sulfuric acid solution is an irritant.
- Ethanol is harmful.
- 2,4-dinitrophenylhydrazine is toxic by inhalation and is dangerous to the environment. It can cause explosions when dry.

Record your observations here.

Analysis of results

● What do you notice about the products from the test with 2,4-DNPH?

....

....

● Compare the melting point of your pure 2,4-DNPH derivative with the melting points shown
in the table and identify the unknown carbonyl compound.

....

....

Carbonyl compound	Melting point of derivative/°C
ethanal	168
propanal	155
benzaldehyde	237
propanone	128
butan-2-one	115
4-methylphenylethanone	258

Questions

1 What type of reaction occurs between the carbonyl compound and 2,4-DNPH?

....

2 Why is it necessary to recrystallise the sample?

....

....

3 Why should the impure solid be dissolved in the minimum volume of hot solvent?

....

....

....

....

4 What would happen to the melting point if the pure crystals were not completely dry?

....

....

5 Which methods of spectroscopy might you use as alternatives to determine which carbonyl compound you have?

....

....

6 Explain how each method will enable the identification of the compound.

....

....

....

....

....

....

....

....

....

....

....

Practical 23 Follow the rate of the iodine–propanone reaction using a titrimetric method

PAG 9

CPAC links		Evidence	Done
1a	Correctly follows instructions to carry out the experimental techniques or procedures.	Practical procedure	
2a	Correctly uses appropriate instrumentation, apparatus and materials (including ICT) to carry out investigative activities, experimental techniques and procedures with minimal assistance or prompting.	Practical procedure	
2b	Carries out techniques or procedures methodically, in sequence and in combination, identifying practical issues and making adjustments when necessary.	Practical procedure	
3b	Uses appropriate safety equipment and approaches to minimise risks with minimal prompting.	Practical procedure	
4b	Obtains accurate, precise and sufficient data for experimental and investigative procedures and records this methodically using appropriate units and conventions.	Practical procedure and results table	

Procedure

1 Mix 25 cm^3 of 1 mol dm^{-3} aqueous propanone with 25 cm^3 of 1 mol dm^{-3} sulfuric acid in a beaker.

2 Start the stop clock the moment you add 50 cm^3 of 0.02 mol dm^{-3} iodine solution. Shake the beaker to mix well.

3 Using a pipette, withdraw a 10 cm^3 sample of the mixture and transfer it to a conical flask.

4 Stop the reaction by adding a spatula measure of sodium hydrogencarbonate. Note the exact time at which the sodium hydrogencarbonate is added.

5 Titrate the remaining iodine present in the sample with 0.01 mol dm^{-3} sodium thiosulfate(VI) solution, using starch indicator. Record your results in the table in the analysis section.

6 Continue to withdraw 10 cm^3 samples at suitable time intervals (approximately every 5 minutes) and treat them similarly. Always note the exact time at which the sodium hydrogencarbonate is added.

Learning tips

- The reaction between propanone and iodine in aqueous solution can be catalysed by an acid:

  $I_2(aq) + CH_3COCH_3(aq) + H^+(aq) \rightarrow CH_3COCH_2I(aq) + 2H^+(aq) + I^-(aq)$

- The influence of the iodine on the reaction rate can be studied if the concentrations of propanone and hydrogen ions effectively remain constant during the reaction. This is achieved by using a large excess of both propanone and sulfuric acid in the starting reaction mixture.

Objectives

- To determine the rate of a reaction using a continuous monitoring method
- To determine the order of reaction with respect to a substance using a concentration–time graph

Equipment

- 50 cm^3 of 1 mol dm^{-3} aqueous propanone solution
- 50 cm^3 of 1 mol dm^{-3} sulfuric acid
- 50 cm^3 of 0.02 mol dm^{-3} iodine solution (in 0.2 mol dm^{-3} potassium iodide solution)
- 0.01 mol dm^{-3} sodium thiosulfate(VI) solution
- 20 cm^3 of 1% starch solution/indicator
- sodium hydrogencarbonate
- 100 cm^3 beaker
- conical flasks
- 10 cm^3 graduated pipettes
- pipette filler
- spatula
- stop clock

Safety

- Wear eye protection.
- Sodium thiosulfate releases sulfur dioxide when it reacts. Ensure that the room is well-ventilated.
- Propanone is an irritant and is highly flammable.
- Sulfuric acid solution is an irritant.

Write your results in the table.

Time hydrogencarbonate added/min					
Initial reading/cm³					
Final reading/cm³					
Titre/cm³					

Analysis of results

Plot a graph of titre against time. (The titre is proportional to the concentration of iodine.)

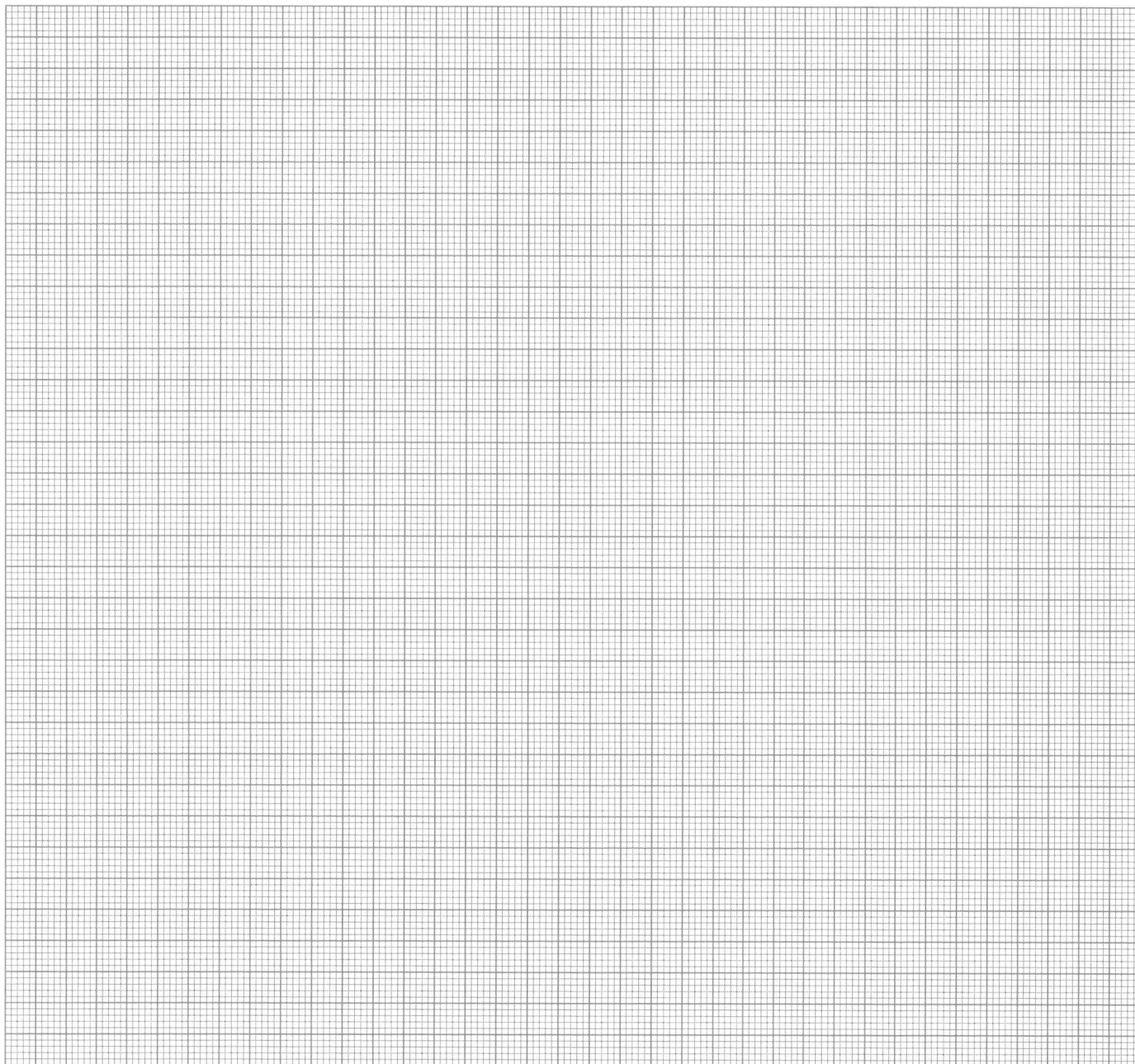

● Describe in words how the rate changes as the concentration of iodine changes.

....

....

- Deduce the order of reaction with respect to iodine from the graph.

....

....

Conclusion

Interpret your findings and write a conclusion to discuss your results.

....

....

....

....

....

....

....

Questions

Similar experiments show that the reaction is first order with respect to both propanone and to hydrogen ions. Use this information to answer the following questions.

1 What is the effect on the rate if the concentration of the hydrogen ions is doubled?

....

2 What is the effect on the rate if the concentration of the propanone is doubled?

....

3 What is the effect on the rate if the concentration of the iodine is doubled?

....

4 Give the overall rate expression for this reaction.

....

....

5 Two students monitored the concentration of propanone as the reaction proceeded and plotted a concentration–time graph from their results.

What shape would you expect the graph to be? How would you use this graph to prove that the reaction is first order with respect to propanone?

....

....

....

....

....

....

PAG 6

CPAC links		Evidence	Done
1a	Correctly follows instructions to carry out the experimental techniques or procedures.	Practical procedure	
2a	Correctly uses appropriate instrumentation, apparatus and materials (including ICT) to carry out investigative activities, experimental techniques and procedures with minimal assistance or prompting.	Practical procedure	
2b	Carries out techniques or procedures methodically, in sequence and in combination, identifying practical issues and making adjustments when necessary.	Practical procedure and answers to questions	
3b	Uses appropriate safety equipment and approaches to minimise risks with minimal prompting.	Practical procedure	
4a	Makes accurate observations relevant to the experimental or investigative procedure.	Measurements and results table	

Objectives

- To use two chromatographic techniques
- To identify amino acids in a mixture using thin layer chromatography (TLC) and paper chromatography

Equipment

- 1% solutions of glycine, leucine, proline, serine and valine
- mixture of amino acids
- chromatography paper 21.5 cm × 11 cm
- paper clips
- prepared solvent containing butanol, ethanoic acid and water
- TLC cellulose slide
- ninhydrin spray (used by teacher only)
- chromatography tank and lid, or large gas jar and lid
- capillary tubes
- warm oven or hair dryer

Safety

- Wear eye protection.
- Perform the experiment in a well-ventilated room.
- Ninhydrin spray is harmful – it should only be used in a fume cupboard by your teacher.
- The prepared solvent is highly flammable, harmful and corrosive.

Procedure

This experiment is to be performed using chromatography paper and a thin layer slide so that the two methods can be compared.

Chromatography paper method

1. Draw a pencil line across the chromatography paper about 1.5 cm from the bottom. Mark six spots on the line with a pencil. This is where you are going to apply each amino acid and the mixture. Label the six spots.

2. Select an amino acid and, using a capillary tube, put one spot of the amino acid on the paper at its allocated point.

3. Let the spot dry and then add another spot of the *same* amino acid in the *same* place.

4. Repeat steps 2 and 3 with the other amino acids until you have applied all five along the line.

5. Now apply the amino acid mixture to the sixth place.

6. Pour some solvent into the chromatography container or gas jar so that it *just covers* the bottom of the container.

7. Hang the paper in the container (or roll the paper so that it forms a cylinder and put a paper clip at the top to hold it in place) and then put it in the gas jar. The solvent must be *below* the pencil line.

8. Cover the container or gas jar.

9. Run the chromatogram until the solvent has moved at least 10 cm up the paper. Remove the paper from the container and mark where the solvent reached with a pencil line.

10. Allow the paper to dry.

11. The paper must now be sprayed with ninhydrin by your teacher. Put the paper in a warm oven (or dry with a hairdryer) to help the spots to develop.

Thin layer slide method

1   Draw a small mark on the thin layer slide about 1.5 cm from the bottom on the left-hand side.

2   Apply the individual amino acids and the mixture in line with the mark – as with paper chromatography.

3   Put the slide into the chromatography container (or gas jar) with the same solvent and replace the lid.

4   Allow the solvent to rise the same distance as on the paper chromatogram. Remove the slide from the container and mark the position of the solvent front.

5   Follow steps 10 and 11 in the chromatography paper method.

Record your results and calculations here.

Analysis of results

● Measure the distance travelled by the solvent from pencil line to pencil line.

● Measure the distance travelled by each amino acid (from the lower pencil line to the centre of the spot).

● Find the R_f (retardation factor) value of each amino acid using the relationship:

$$R_f = \frac{\text{distance travelled by amino acid}}{\text{distance travelled by the solvent}}$$

● Calculate the R_f values of the spots in the mixture.

● Compare the R_f values and decide which amino acids were present in the mixture.

Questions

1   Why is ninhydrin used?

....

....

....

2   What would happen if the solvent level was higher than the applied spots of solute when the chromatogram was
    put into the container?

....

....

3   What are the stationary phases and the mobile phases in the paper chromatography and TLC methods?

....

....

....

....

....

4   By what process does the solute move up the paper? What process is happening during TLC?

....

....

....

....

5   Why does the container have to be covered?

....

....

....

6   What advantages does TLC have compared to paper chromatography?

....

....

....

....

PAG 6

CPAC links		Evidence	Done
1a	Correctly follows instructions to carry out the experimental techniques or procedures.	Practical procedure	
2a	Correctly uses appropriate instrumentation, apparatus and materials (including ICT) to carry out investigative activities, experimental techniques and procedures with minimal assistance or prompting.	Practical procedure	
2b	Carries out techniques or procedures methodically, in sequence and in combination, identifying practical issues and making adjustments when necessary.	Practical procedure and answers to questions	
2d	Selects appropriate equipment and measurement strategies in order to ensure suitably accurate results.	Answers to questions	
3b	Uses appropriate safety equipment and approaches to minimise risks with minimal prompting.	Practical procedure	
4b	Obtains accurate, precise and sufficient data for experimental and investigative procedures and records this methodically using appropriate units and conventions.	Measurements and results table	

Diagram

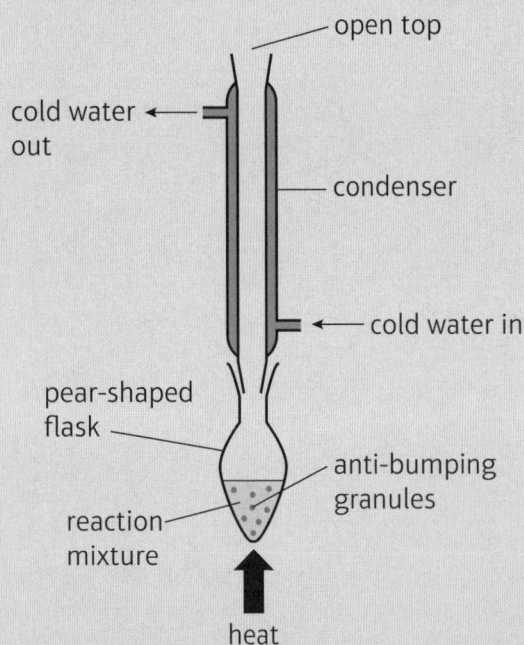

Figure A. Apparatus for heating under reflux

Objectives
- To manipulate materials and equipment with care and precision
- To hydrolyse an ester and produce a high yield of pure product

Equipment
- 3 cm³ of methyl benzoate
- 10 cm³ of 2 mol dm⁻³ sodium hydroxide solution
- 20 cm³ of 2 mol dm⁻³ hydrochloric acid solution
- 10 cm³ of ethanol
- methyl orange indicator
- 50 cm³ round-bottomed flask (*Quickfit®*)
- water-cooled condenser (to fit flask) with rubber tubing
- four 10 cm³ measuring cylinders
- anti-bumping granules
- Bunsen burner, safety mat and splints
- two 100 cm³ beakers
- stirring rod and spatula
- mass balance (2 d.p.) and weighing boats
- Büchner funnel, Büchner flask with water (suction) pump and filter paper to fit funnel
- melting point apparatus and melting point tubes
- stand, clamp and boss
- kettles for boiling water
- dropping pipettes

Safety
- Wear a lab coat, eye protection and disposable nitrile gloves.
- Tie long hair back.
- Methyl benzoate is harmful by inhalation. Perform the experiment in a well-ventilated room.
- 2 mol dm⁻³ sodium hydroxide is corrosive.
- Ethanol is highly flammable – keep away from flames.
- 2 mol dm⁻³ hydrochloric acid solution and benzoic acid are irritants.

Procedure

1 Measure 3 cm³ of methyl benzoate and pour it into a 50 cm³ round-bottomed flask.

2 Add 10 cm³ of 2 mol dm⁻³ sodium hydroxide solution and 10 cm³ of ethanol to the flask.

3 Add a few anti-bumping granules and then fix a water-cooled condenser to the flask ready for refluxing.

4 Heat the flask gently, slowly bringing the contents to the boil. Reflux for 20 minutes.

5 Allow the contents of the flask to cool with the condenser still in place. When cool, remove the condenser from the flask and decant the contents of the flask into the 100 cm³ beaker.

6 Add 4–5 drops of methyl orange indicator and stir the solution. Acidify with 1 cm³ portions of hydrochloric acid solution, stirring after each addition. This process should use less than 20 cm³ of HCl(aq).

7 Filter the solid product under reduced pressure.

8 Recrystallise the product (benzoic acid) using the minimum volume of boiling water. Filter the purified benzoic acid under reduced pressure and allow it to dry in the air.

9 When dry, weigh the benzoic acid and record its mass in the space below.

10 Using some of the dry sample, use melting point apparatus to measure the melting point of the benzoic acid. Record its melting point.

Learning tip

$$\text{Percentage yield} = \frac{\text{actual yield}}{\text{expected yield}} \times 100$$

Record your observations here.

Analysis of results

1   Calculate the mass of the 3 cm³ sample of methyl benzoate used.

....

....

....

....

....

2   Use the given equations and your yield of benzoic acid to calculate the percentage yield.

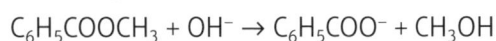

$$C_6H_5COOCH_3 + OH^- \rightarrow C_6H_5COO^- + CH_3OH$$

$$C_6H_5COO^- + H^+ \rightarrow C_6H_5COOH$$

H = 1.0, C = 12.0 and O = 16.0

The density of methyl benzoate is 1.09 g cm⁻³

....

....

....

....

....

....

....

....

Questions

1   In Step 4, why is the reaction mixture heated under reflux?

....

....

....

....

....

2   Why is the solution acidified in Step 6?

....

....

....

....

3 Explain why ethanoic acid is soluble in water and why benzoic acid is insoluble in cold water.

4 Explain why the benzoic acid should be purified by recrystallisation in the **minimum** amount of boiling water.

5 Explain why recrystallisation should produce a purer product.

6 Suggest what might be the most significant source of measurement uncertainty and suggest a modification to reduce this uncertainty.

7 Give two reasons why your percentage yield is lower than 100%.

PAG 10

CPAC links		Evidence	Done
1a	Correctly follows instructions to carry out the experimental techniques or procedures.	Practical procedure	
2a	Correctly uses appropriate instrumentation, apparatus and materials (including ICT) to carry out investigative activities, experimental techniques and procedures with minimal assistance or prompting.	Practical procedure	
2b	Carries out techniques or procedures methodically, in sequence and in combination, identifying practical issues and making adjustments when necessary.	Practical procedure	
3b	Uses appropriate safety equipment and approaches to minimise risks with minimal prompting.	Practical procedure	
4b	Obtains accurate, precise and sufficient data for experimental and investigative procedures and records this methodically using appropriate units and conventions.	Measurements and results table	
5a	Uses appropriate software and/ or tools to process data, carry out research and report findings.	Processing of data	

Objective

- To use the Arrhenius equation to determine the activation energy of a reaction

Equipment

- $70 \, cm^3$ of $0.01 \, mol \, dm^{-3}$ aqueous phenol solution
- $70 \, cm^3$ of bromide/bromate solution
- $50 \, cm^3$ of $0.5 \, mol \, dm^{-3}$ sulfuric acid
- methyl red indicator
- three $100 \, cm^3$ beakers
- two boiling tubes
- $10 \, cm^3$ pipette
- thermometer (0–110 °C)
- stop clock
- $500 \, cm^3$ beaker
- kettle

Safety

- Wear safety goggles, a lab coat and gloves.
- Phenol is corrosive and toxic.
- Sulfuric acid solution is an irritant.
- Potassium bromate(V) is oxidising.

Procedure

1 Pipette $10 \, cm^3$ of phenol solution and $10 \, cm^3$ of bromide/bromate solution into the same boiling tube.

2 Add four drops of methyl red indicator to the mixture.

3 Pipette $5 \, cm^3$ of sulfuric acid solution into another boiling tube.

4 Use a kettle and a beaker to prepare a water bath with a temperature of 75 °C (±1 °C). Immerse the two boiling tubes in the water bath.

5 When the contents of the boiling tubes have reached the water temperature, mix the contents of the two tubes by pouring rapidly from one tube to the other and back again. Start the stop clock at the same time.

6 Leave the boiling tube containing the reaction mixture in the water, and time until the methyl red indicator disappears.

7 Use the first two columns of the results table below to record all your results.

8 Repeat the whole experiment at 65, 55, 45, 35, 25 and 15 °C. Use ice to achieve the lowest temperature.

Learning tips

- The Arrhenius equation is an exponential relationship between the rate constant, k, and temperature, T:

$k = Ae^{-\frac{E_a}{RT}}$

where R = gas constant = 8.314 J mol^{-1} K^{-1}

T = temperature in Kelvin

E_a = activation energy of the reaction

$k \propto$ reaction rate $\propto \dfrac{1}{t}$ so we can say that

$k = \dfrac{\text{a constant}}{\text{time taken for methyl red to bleach}} = \dfrac{c}{t}$

- The Arrhenius equation can also be expressed as a logarithmic relationship:

$\ln k = -\dfrac{E_a}{RT} + \ln A$ or $\ln\left(\dfrac{c}{t}\right) = -\dfrac{E_a}{RT} + \ln A$

Rearranging: $\ln t = \ln c - \ln A + \dfrac{E_a}{RT}$

$\ln c$ and $\ln A$ are constants, so a graph of $\ln t$ against $\dfrac{1}{T}$ has a gradient of $\dfrac{E_a}{R}$.

Record your results here.

$T/°C$	Time, t/s	T/K	$\frac{1}{T}/K^{-1}$	$\ln t$

Analysis of results

- Calculate temperatures in Kelvin, K, and fill in the third column of the table (0 °C = 273 K).
- Fill in the fourth column of the table by dividing each of the temperatures into 1.
- Fill in the fifth column by taking natural logs of the times.
- Plot a graph of $\ln t$ (y-axis) against $\dfrac{1}{T}$ (x-axis).

Plot your graph here.

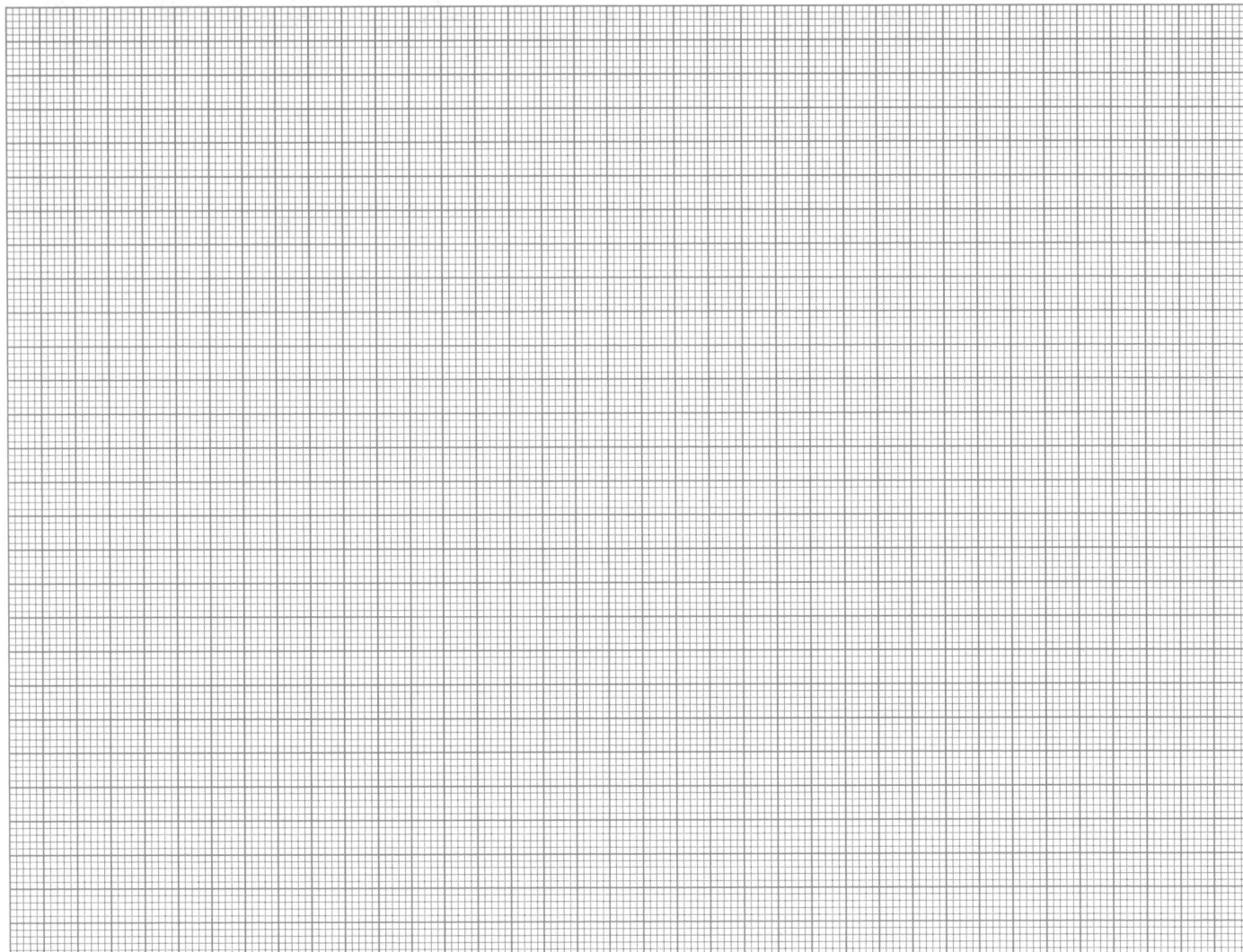

Questions

1 Write an equation for the reaction between bromine and phenol.

....

....

2 What function does the methyl red have in this experiment?

....

....

....

3 Measure the gradient of your graph.

....

....

4 Calculate the activation energy of the reaction, E_a.

....

....

....

PAG 11

CPAC links		Evidence	Done
2a	Correctly uses appropriate instrumentation, apparatus and materials (including ICT) to carry out investigative activities, experimental techniques and procedures with minimal assistance or prompting.	Practical procedure	
4b	Obtains accurate, precise and sufficient data for experimental and investigative procedures and records this methodically using appropriate units and conventions.	Observations and results table	
5a	Uses appropriate software and/ or tools to process data, carry out research and report findings.	Spreadsheet, graph and answers to calculations	

Procedure

1 Set up the datalogger to read the pH for a given volume of added base. Select *manual sampling*, then select: *keep data only when commanded,* enter a keyboard value when data is kept and prompt for a value. (If your datalogger does not have this capacity you may have to record the volume of added base separately.)

2 Pipette 25 cm³ of 0.1 mol dm⁻³ hydrochloric acid solution into a small beaker.

3 Measure and record the pH of the acid using the pH electrode and the datalogger.

4 Add the following volumes (cm³) of base (0.1 mol dm⁻³ sodium hydroxide solution):

5; 5; 5; 5; 2; 1; 1; 0.5; 0.5; 0.5; 0.5; 1; 1; 2; 5 and 5

The total volume of base added is 40 cm³.

5 After each addition, stir the solution and record the pH of the solution and the volume of base added.

6 Use the data collected and your datalogger to generate the pH curve for HCl/NaOH.

7 Connect the datalogger to a computer and copy the data into a spreadsheet to plot and print the graph.

8 Repeat the procedure using the following combinations of acids and bases:

 • hydrochloric acid and ammonia solutions
 • ethanoic acid and sodium hydroxide solutions
 • ethanoic acid and ammonia solutions.

Objectives

 • To follow an acid–base titration by measuring the pH after the addition of different volumes of base to an acid
 • To collect data using a datalogger and use the datalogger to generate a graph

Equipment

 • 75 cm³ of 0.1 mol dm⁻³ hydrochloric acid solution
 • 75 cm³ of 0.1 mol dm⁻³ ethanoic acid solution
 • 100 cm³ of 0.1 mol dm⁻³ sodium hydroxide solution
 • 100 cm³ of 0.1 mol dm⁻³ ammonia solution
 • datalogger and pH probe
 • stand, clamp and boss for pH probe
 • two 50 cm³ burettes
 • two burette stands
 • four 100 cm³ beakers
 • glass rods
 • distilled/deionised water
 • 25 cm³ pipette and filler

Safety

 • Wear a lab coat and use eye protection.
 • Tie long hair back.
 • Sodium hydroxide solution is an irritant.

Print out the spreadsheet and graph and stick them in here.

Questions

1 Write an equation for each titration. Classify each curve according to the strengths of the acid and the base. For example, HCl and NaOH is strong acid–strong base, and CH_3COOH and NH_3 is weak acid–weak base.

....

....

....

....

....

....

....

....

2 For each curve, note the change in pH at equivalence (when the molar ratio of the acid to base is 1 : 1) – this is the pH at the lower and upper points of the steep rise.

....

....

....

....

....

....

....

....

3 Select a suitable indicator for each acid–base curve using the given data.
Indicators and their pH ranges:
methyl orange: 3.1–4.4
alizarin yellow: 10.1–12.0
phenolphthalein: 8.2–10.0
methyl red: 4.2–6.3
bromophenol blue: 2.8–4.6
bromothymol blue: 6.0–7.6
bromocresol green: 3.8–5.4

....

....

....

....

....

4   Why is it difficult to select an indicator for the weak acid–weak base curve?

....

....

....

....

5   Calculate the pH of a 0.075 mol dm^{-3} solution of sulfuric acid, assuming it to be fully ionised.

....

....

....

....

6   A total of 25 cm^3 of ammonia solution is added in small portions to 10 cm^3 of 0.075 mol dm^{-3} sulfuric acid solution. Equivalence occurs when 20 cm^3 of ammonia solution has been added. Sketch a graph to show how the pH changes during this titration.

PAG 11

CPAC links		Evidence	Done
1a	Correctly follows instructions to carry out the experimental techniques or procedures.	Practical procedure	
2a	Correctly uses appropriate instrumentation, apparatus and materials (including ICT) to carry out investigative activities, experimental techniques and procedures with minimal assistance or prompting.	Practical procedure	
2b	Carries out techniques or procedures methodically, in sequence and in combination, identifying practical issues and making adjustments when necessary.	Practical procedure and answers to questions	
4b	Obtains accurate, precise and sufficient data for experimental and investigative procedures and records this methodically using appropriate units and conventions.	Measurements and results table	

Objective
- To determine K_a for a weak acid

Equipment
- $75\,cm^3$ of $0.1\,mol\,dm^{-3}$ ethanoic acid solution
- $100\,cm^3$ of $0.1\,mol\,dm^{-3}$ sodium hydroxide solution
- datalogger and pH probe or pH meter
- stand, clamp and boss for pH probe
- $50\,cm^3$ burette
- burette stand
- $250\,cm^3$ conical flask
- $25\,cm^3$ pipette and filler
- phenolphthalein indicator

Safety
- Wear a lab coat and use eye protection.
- Tie long hair back.
- Sodium hydroxide solution is an irritant.

Procedure
1. Set up the datalogger to read pH, or calibrate the pH meter.
2. Pipette $25\,cm^3$ of $0.1\,mol\,dm^{-3}$ ethanoic acid solution into a $250\,cm^3$ conical flask.
3. Fill a burette with sodium hydroxide solution.
4. Add two or three drops of phenolphthalein to the conical flask.
5. Titrate the ethanoic acid with sodium hydroxide solution until the mixture just turns red.
6. Pipette a further $25\,cm^3$ of $0.1\,mol\,dm^{-3}$ ethanoic acid solution into the $250\,cm^3$ conical flask.
7. Record the pH of this solution.

Learning tips
- The ionisation of an acid is shown by:

  $$HA(aq) \rightleftharpoons H^+(aq) + A^-(aq)$$

  Because there is an equilibrium set up, an equilibrium constant, K_a, can be written:

  $$K_a = \frac{[H^+][A^-]}{[HA]}$$

- The K_a value is an indication of acid strength. The larger the value of the K_a, the stronger the acid.
- The K_a of a weak acid can be measured by titrating a known volume of the acid against sodium hydroxide using phenolphthalein as an indicator. A further equal volume of acid is then added, and the pH of the resulting solution measured. Because effectively half of the acid has been titrated:

  $$[H^+] = [HA] = [A^-]$$

  $[A^-]$ and $[HA]$ can be cancelled in $K_a = \frac{[H^+][A^-]}{[HA]}$

  $$K_a = [H^+]$$

Record your results here.

Questions

1 Use the pH of your solution to calculate [H⁺].

....

....

....

2 Calculate a value of K_a for ethanoic acid.

....

....

....

3 What are some of the potential sources of uncertainty in this experiment? What can you do to overcome them?

....

....

....

....

....

....

....

PAG 7

CPAC links		Evidence	Done
1a	Correctly follows instructions to carry out the experimental techniques or procedures.	Practical procedure	
3b	Uses appropriate safety equipment and approaches to minimise risks with minimal prompting.	Practical procedure	
4a	Makes accurate observations relevant to the experimental or investigative procedure.	Practical procedure	

Objective

- To know the characteristic reactions of carboxylic acids

Equipment

- $3\,cm^3$ of glacial ethanoic acid
- $3\,cm^3$ of $1\,mol\,dm^{-3}$ ethanoic acid solution
- $5\,cm^3$ of $0.5\,mol\,dm^{-3}$ sodium hydroxide solution
- solid sodium carbonate
- magnesium ribbon
- $10\,cm^3$ of $0.5\,mol\,dm^{-3}$ sodium carbonate solution
- $2\,cm^3$ of limewater
- $1\,cm^3$ of concentrated sulfuric acid
- $1\,cm^3$ of ethanol
- universal indicator solution and paper
- ten test tubes and test tube rack
- $100\,cm^3$ beaker
- distilled/deionised water
- dropping pipettes
- Bunsen burner and safety mat
- spatula
- three $10\,cm^3$ measuring cylinders

Procedure

1. Record all the observations for each test tube reaction in the space below. Add $0.5\,cm^3$ of glacial ethanoic acid to $1\,cm^3$ of distilled/deionised water in a test tube, followed by four to five drops of universal indicator solution. What is the pH of the mixture?

2. Add $1\,cm^3$ of $1\,mol\,dm^{-3}$ ethanoic acid solution to a piece of magnesium ribbon in a test tube. What do you see? Test the gas produced with a lighted splint.

3. Add a few drops of universal indicator to $1\,cm^3$ of $1\,mol\,dm^{-3}$ ethanoic acid solution in a test tube. Add sodium hydroxide drop-wise to the ethanoic acid.

4. Add a spatula measure of sodium carbonate powder to $1\,cm^3$ of $1\,mol\,dm^{-3}$ ethanoic acid in a test tube. Test the gas produced by bubbling it through limewater.

5. Combine $1\,cm^3$ of glacial ethanoic acid with $1\,cm^3$ of ethanol in a test tube. Add two drops of concentrated sulfuric acid to the mixture. Boil gently. Pour the mixture into a small beaker containing some sodium carbonate solution. Smell the mixture. What does it remind you of?

Safety

- Perform the experiment in a well-ventilated room.
- Wear a lab coat, eye protection and disposable nitrile gloves.
- Tie long hair back.
- Ethanoic acid, ethanoic anhydride, concentrated sulfuric acid and sodium hydroxide solution are corrosive.
- Ethanol and magnesium are highly flammable.
- Ethanoic acid solution is an irritant.

Record your observations here.

Describe your observations and identify the products of each reaction in Steps 2–4.

Questions

1   Write equations for the reactions you observed in Steps 2–4.

....

....

....

2   The reactions of ethanoic acid in Steps 1–4 are similar to those of hydrochloric acid. Give two pieces of evidence to suggest that ethanoic acid is a weak acid.

....

....

....

....

3   What type of reaction occurs between ethanoic acid and ethanol? Write an equation for the reaction.

....

....

PAG 12

CPAC links		Evidence	Done
2a	Correctly uses appropriate instrumentation, apparatus and materials (including ICT) to carry out investigative activities, experimental techniques and procedures with minimal assistance or prompting.	Planning and practical procedure	
2c	Identifies and controls significant quantitative variables where applicable, and plans approaches to take account of variables that cannot readily be controlled.	Planning and practical procedure	
2d	Selects appropriate equipment and measurement strategies in order to ensure suitably accurate results.	Planning	
3a	Identifies hazards and assesses risks associated with these hazards, making safety adjustments as necessary, when carrying out experimental techniques and procedures in the lab or field.	Risk assessment	
5b	Sources of information are cited demonstrating that research has taken place, supporting planning and conclusions.	Planning with citations	

Objectives

- To research the tests for ions and organic compounds
- To test unknown substances to establish their identity

- concentrated hydrochloric acid
- 1 mol dm^{-3} sodium hydroxide
- 1 mol dm^{-3} nitric acid
- 0.1 mol dm^{-3} silver nitrate solution
- 1 mol dm^{-3} ammonia solution
- 1 mol dm^{-3} dilute hydrochloric acid
- barium chloride solution
- limewater
- bromine water
- sodium carbonate solution
- ethanol
- concentrated sulfuric acid
- four tubs labelled A, B, C, D
- three bottles labelled X, Y, Z
- nichrome wire
- delivery tube
- Bunsen burner and heat-proof mat
- test tubes and bungs
- distilled water
- dropping pipettes
- spatulas
- boiling tube
- 250 cm^3 beaker
- 100 cm^3 beaker
- access to a kettle

Procedure

Identifying inorganic ions

1. Look up how to carry out the flame test to identify metal cations.

2. Write a plan for the safe conduct of a flame-test experiment. You should describe in detail how you would carry out the experiment and the results you would expect.

3. Look up how to use sodium hydroxide to identify metal cations.

4. Write a plan for the safe conduct of this sodium hydroxide experiment. You should describe in detail how you would carry out the experiment and the results you would expect.

5. Look up how to use silver nitrate to identify halide ions.

6. Write a plan for the safe conduct of this silver nitrate experiment. You should describe in detail how you would carry out the experiment and the results you would expect.

Safety

- Wear eye protection.
- Tie long hair back.
- Concentrated hydrochloric acid, sodium hydroxide and concentrated sulfuric acid are corrosive.
- Nitric acid, hydrochloric acid and limewater are irritants.
- Barium chloride and bromine water are toxic and irritants.
- Ethanol is flammable – do not use it near a lit Bunsen burner.
- Pay attention to the hazard warnings on the tubs and bottles of unknown substances.
  In particular, if anything is marked flammable do not use/store it anywhere near a lit Bunsen burner. If you need to heat a flammable substance, you *must* do this by standing the substance in a beaker of hot water.

7   Look up how to test for sulfate ions.

8   Write a plan for the safe conduct of this experiment to test for sulfate ions. You should describe in detail how you would carry out the experiment and the results you would expect.

9   Look up how to test for carbonate ions.

10 Write a plan for the safe conduct of this experiment to test for carbonate ions. You should describe in detail how you would carry out the experiment and the results you would expect.

11 Carry out your experiments to identify substances A–D. Pay particular attention to the management of safety.

Write your plans for identifying inorganic ions here, then get them checked.

Include safety notes and remember to cite the sources of information.

Record your observations for substances A–D here.

Organic analysis

1 Look up how to test for alkenes.

2 Write a plan for the safe conduct of this experiment to test for an alkene. You should describe in detail how you would carry out the experiment and the results you would expect.

3 Look up how to test for an aldehyde.

4 Write a plan for the safe conduct of this experiment to test for an aldehyde. You should describe in detail how you would carry out the experiment and the results you would expect.

5 Look up how to test for carboxylic acids.

6 Write a plan for the safe conduct of this experiment to test for carboxylic acids. You should describe in detail how you would carry out the experiment and the results that you would expect.

7 Carry out your experiments to identify substances X–Z. Take appropriate safety precautions.

Write your plans for organic analysis here, then get them checked.

Record your observations for substances X–Z here.

Questions

1 When testing an inorganic compound for the presence of halide ions, why is nitric acid added before adding silver nitrate?

....

....

2 What further test could you do to distinguish between sulfate(VI) ions and sulfate(IV) ions?

....

....

3 Outline a further test you could use to identify the presence of an aldehyde group.

....

....

....

Practical 1
Plan
Your **risk assessment** must include the following points:
- Do not look directly at burning magnesium.
- Wear eye protection.
- Magnesium is highly flammable.
- The crucible and lid will become hot during heating and should be handled with tongs.

Your **equipment list** should include:
- Bunsen burner, tripod, pipeclay triangle, heat-resistant mat
- crucible and lid
- tongs
- magnesium ribbon
- small piece of sand paper
- mass balance accurate to 2 d.p.

Your **procedure** should cover the following points:
1 Weigh the empty crucible with its lid and record the result.
2 Use the sandpaper to clean the piece of magnesium ribbon.
3 Coil the magnesium loosely around a pencil. Put the magnesium ribbon into the crucible and put the lid on.
4 Weigh the crucible, lid and magnesium. Write the result in your table.
5 Put the crucible onto the pipeclay triangle. Heat the crucible gently for one minute, then heat it more strongly. Lift the lid from time to time, to allow air in, but try not to let any of the white smoke escape.
6 Once the reaction is complete, the magnesium ribbon will stop glowing. At this point, turn the Bunsen burner off. Allow the crucible to cool for a few minutes.
7 Reweigh the crucible with its lid and contents, and write the result in your table.

Results
Your results table should look something like this:

	Mass/g
Crucible and lid before heating	
Crucible, lid and magnesium ribbon before heating	
Crucible, lid and magnesium ribbon after heating	
Mass of magnesium	
Mass of oxygen	

Sample data is shown below.
You can use these data to calculate the mass of magnesium used in the experiment and the mass of oxygen the magnesium reacted with. You can then calculate the relative atomic mass of each element and use this information to calculate the number of moles of each element.

Finally, you can calculate the ratio of the combining elements by dividing the number of moles of each element by the smaller value.

Sample data

	Mass/g
Crucible and lid before heating	51.54
Crucible, lid and magnesium ribbon before heating	62.63
Crucible, lid and magnesium ribbon after heating	70.02
Mass of magnesium	11.09
Mass of oxygen	7.4

Sample data is shown below.

	Magnesium, Mg	Oxygen, O
Mass of element	11.09	7.40
A_r of element	24	16
Number of moles	0.46	0.46
Ratio of elements	$\frac{0.46}{0.46} = 1$	$\frac{0.46}{0.46} = 1$

Answers to questions
1 The formula that represents the simplest ratio of atoms in an element.
2 MgO
3 MgO
4 $2Mg + O_2 \rightarrow 2MgO$

Practical 2
Sample data

	Hydrochloric acid	Sulfuric acid	Ethanoic acid	Citric acid
CuO	black solid dissolves to give clear blue solution	black solid dissolves to give clear blue solution	black solid partially dissolves to give clear blue solution	no reaction
MgO	white solid dissolves to give colourless solution	white solid dissolves to give colourless solution	white solid partially dissolves	no reaction
NaOH	colourless solution forms, test tube feels warm	colourless solution forms, test tube feels warm	colourless solution forms, test tube feels warm	colourless solution forms
NH_3	colourless solution forms, test tube feels warm	colourless solution forms, test tube feels warm	no visible reaction	no reaction
$CuCO_3$	solid dissolves, effervescence and blue solution forms, gas produced turns limewater cloudy	solid dissolves, effervescence and blue solution forms, gas produced turns limewater cloudy	fizzing, gas produced turns limewater slightly cloudy	small amount of fizzing
$CaCO_3$	solid dissolves, effervescence, gas produced turns limewater cloudy	solid dissolves, effervescence, gas produced turns limewater cloudy	fizzing, gas produced turns limewater slightly cloudy	small amount of fizzing

Answers to questions
1 Weak substances have fewer H^+ or OH^- ions available for reaction, so less energy is released. Weak substances will eventually react fully, but an energy input is required to complete the dissociation.
2 Above $0.4\,mol\,dm^{-3}$, NaOH becomes corrosive and attacks fat molecules in the skin.
3 Calcium carbonate, magnesium carbonate and magnesium hydroxide. These substances have a lower pH than the other alkalis so they are not corrosive.
4 Vinegar, because the ethanoic acid will neutralise the alkali in the sting.

Practical 3
Sample data
Mass of metal = 0.2 g
Volume of hydrogen gas collected = $200\,cm^3$

Answers to questions

1 A major procedural error is the loss of hydrogen gas. The stopper must be replaced in the conical flask as quickly as possible.

2 Putting the powder and the acid in a dual compartment flask.

3 Amount of $X = \dfrac{0.20}{24.3} = 0.0082 \, mol$

Amount of HCl needed = $0.0082 \times 2 = 0.0164 \, mol$

Amount of HCl used = $1.00 \times \dfrac{25.0}{1000} = 0.025 \, mol$

This is greater than 0.0164 so the HCl is in excess.

4 Pour the acid into the flask first and then add the lump of metal.

5 Use water instead of hydrochloric acid.

Practical 4
Answers to questions

1 Added the last $1 \, cm^3$ of water dropwise with a pipette; ensured the meniscus was on the line when read at eye level; inverted the flask several times.

2 Burette – HCl; pipette – sodium carbonate solution; conical flask – distilled water.

3 Determining the end point is usually the main source of procedural error when carrying out a titration. Use a white tile to see the colour change more clearly to try to eliminate this error.

4 0.24%

5 The answer will depend on your average titre but should be approximately $0.2 \, cm^3$.

Practical 5
Sample data

Cyclohexane colours

	KCl	KBr	KI
Chlorine, Cl_2	–	orange	purple
Bromine, Br_2	orange	–	purple
Iodine, I_2	purple	purple	–

Answers to questions

1 Cl > Br > I

2 A chlorine atom has the smallest radius, so its outer orbital is closest to the nucleus and its outer electrons are most strongly attracted to the nucleus. Chlorine also has the smallest electron shielding. As you move down the halogen group, the atomic radius increases. This means that the electron shielding increases as well, so the halogens become less able to attract and gain an extra electron to form a halide ion.

3 $Cl_2(aq) + 2KI(aq) \rightarrow I_2(aq) + 2KCl(aq)$

4 $Cl_2 + 2I^- \rightarrow I_2 + 2Cl^-$

5 a $Cl_2 + 2KAt \rightarrow At_2 + 2KCl$

  b There is no reaction because astatine is less reactive than iodine.

Practical 6
Plan

Your **risk assessment** must include the following points:
- Wear eye protection.
- Dilute ammonia is low hazard.
- Dilute nitric(V) acid is corrosive.
- Concentrated ammonia is corrosive and dangerous to the environment. Use in a fume cupboard.

Your **equipment list** should include:
- $0.1 \, mol \, dm^{-3}$ silver nitrate solution
- dilute ammonia solution
- deionised water
- concentrated ammonia solution
- potassium chloride solution (A)
- potassium bromide solution (B)
- potassium iodide solution (C)
- dilute nitric acid
- unknown solid A15
- unknown solid B15

- spatula
- five test tubes with stoppers
- test tube rack or large beaker
- dropping pipettes
- Your procedure should cover the following points:

1 Take three test tubes and label them A, B and C.

2 Pour $1 \, cm^3$ of each unknown halide solution into the corresponding test tube.

3 Add silver nitrate dropwise to test tube A until a precipitate forms.

4 Add twice the volume of dilute ammonia solution to the test tube, stopper and shake.

5 If the precipitate remains, repeat steps 1 and 2, and then add a few drops of concentrated ammonia solution (in the fume cupboard) and shake carefully (do not stopper).

6 Repeat steps 3–5 for test tubes B and C.

7 Now test the unknown solids A15 and B15 for the presence of halide ions.

8 You will have to make solutions of the solids first. You can use dilute nitric acid to dissolve them, if they do not dissolve in deionised water.

Sample data

Halide	Silver chloride	Silver bromide	Silver iodide
Observations on addition of silver nitrate	white precipitate	cream precipitate	yellow precipitate
Observations on addition of ammonia	dissolves in dilute ammonia	dissolves in concentrated ammonia	insoluble in concentrated ammonia

Answers to questions

1 $AgNO_3 + KCl \rightarrow AgCl + KNO_3$

AgCl is a white precipitate, soluble in dilute ammonia.

$AgNO_3 + KBr \rightarrow AgBr + KNO_3$

AgBr is a cream precipitate, soluble in concentrated ammonia.

$AgNO_3 + KI \rightarrow AgI + KNO_3$

AgI is a pale yellow precipitate, partially soluble/insoluble in concentrated ammonia.

2 Ionic bonding; it is present in compounds containing a metal (Ag) and a non-metal (Cl).

3 $AgNO_3$ would give a precipitate with the chloride and the sulfate ions present in hydrochloric acid and sulfuric acid but the precipitate would not form with nitrate ions in nitric acid.

4 Tap water may contain anions (e.g. chloride ions) that will form a precipitate with the silver ions.

Practical 7
Answers to questions

1 So that any unused zinc stuck in the bottle is taken into account in the calculations.

2 **Advantage:** The graph allows you to read temperatures for times when it was not possible to measure the temperature, e.g. at three minutes.

Disadvantage: the maximum temperature may fall between two readings.

3 Heat loss from equipment; use a better insulated container with a lid.

4 Thermometer = $\dfrac{0.25}{20} \times 100 = 1.25\%$

Pipette = $\dfrac{0.06}{25.0} \times 100 = 0.24\%$

Mass = $\dfrac{0.01}{2.95} \times 100 = 0.34\%$

5 Energy is absorbed to break the metallic bonds in zinc and the hydration bonds of the copper ions. Energy is released in the formation of metallic bonds in copper and the hydration of zinc ions.

Practical 8
Sample data

Time/s	Method 1	Method 2
	Volume of gas/cm³	Mass lost/g
0	0	87.30
10	18	87.24
20	29	87.21
30	36	87.18
40	45	87.16
50	53	87.15
60	63	87.13
70	70	87.12
80	75	87.11
90	79	87.11
100	82	87.10
110	84	87.10
120	88	87.09
150	92	87.09
180	94	87.09
210	96	87.08
240	98	87.08
270	98	87.08
300	98	87.08

Answers to questions

1 The most significant procedural error arises from trying to simultaneously fit the stopper/cotton wool into the test tube/ conical flask, while starting the stop clock and noting the volume in the gas syringe. This error can be minimised if you work in pairs/groups – one of you fits the stopper/cotton wool into the test tube and reads the gas syringe, while another starts the stop clock.

2 Measurement errors:

measuring cylinder $= \frac{1}{20} \times 100 = 5\%$

mass $= \frac{0.01}{10} \times 100 = 0.1\%$

gas syringe varies: for 10 cm³ = 10%; for 72 cm³ = 1.4%

3 Rate = k[HCl]

4 The $CaCO_3$ is a solid and, although its mass decreases, its concentration does not change significantly.

5 $H^+ + CO_3^{2-} \rightarrow HCO_3^-$ slow
$HCO_3^- + H^+ \rightarrow CO_2 + H_2O$ fast

Practical 9
Sample data

Temperature of reaction mixture/°C	Time taken for cross to disappear/s
20	90
30	50
40	25
50	20
55	10

Answers to questions

1 Deciding when the cross has disappeared. Make sure your eyes are the same distance from the reaction mixture, and you are looking at the cross from the same angle each time. Use the same cross each time – do not draw a new one for each experiment, as your crosses will be slightly different.

2 Starting and stopping the stop clock. Working in pairs – with one person pouring while the other starts the stop clock – is a good way to ensure consistency.

3 Repeat the experiment so that you have two or three sets of data.

4 Reaction rate increases with increasing temperature. As a rule of thumb, the rate doubles with every 10 °C increase in temperature.

Practical 10
Sample data

Experiment	Volume Fe(III)/ cm³	Volume KCNS/cm³	Volume water/ cm³	Colour
1	2	18	0	red
2	2	14	4	red
3	2	10	8	red/ orange
4	2	6	12	orange
5	2	2	16	orange

$[Fe(H_2O)_6]^{3+}(aq) + CNS^-(aq) \rightleftharpoons [Fe(H_2O)_5CNS]^{2+}(aq) + H_2O(l)$
orange   blood red

Answers to questions

1 Use a concentration of 0.1 mol dm⁻³ KCNS. Add excess amounts of KCNS to drops of the solution being tested, so that the concentration of KCNS is as high as possible.

2 $2CrO_4^{2-} + 2H^+ \rightleftharpoons Cr_2O_7^{2-} + H_2O$
yellow   orange

3 OH^- ions react with H^+ ions so the concentration of the H^+ ions decreases. To compensate for this, as stated by Le Châtelier's principle, the equilibrium shifts to the left to produce more H^+ ions.

4 The colour of the solution will become orange, because the excess H^+ ions will cause the equilibrium to shift to the right.

Practical 11
Sample data
Cobalt chloride

Effect of warming	Effect of cooling	Effect of adding HCl	Effect of adding water
goes blue	goes pink/red	goes blue	goes pink/red

Copper chloride

Effect of warming	Effect of cooling	Effect of adding HCl	Effect of adding water
goes green	goes blue	goes green	goes blue

Answers to questions

1 a The position of the equilibrium will move left to minimise the increase in H^+ ions.

   b Yellow.

   c There are approximately equal amounts of HIn and In⁻ present at the end point of a titration, so the indicator colour is a mixture of red and yellow (i.e. orange).

2 a The position of the equilibrium moves left to minimise the increase in H^+ ions, producing orange $Cr_2O_7^{2-}$ ions.

   b Hydroxide ions react with H^+ ions, so the position of the equilibrium moves right to minimise the decrease in H^+ ions. This increases the number of CrO_4^{2-} ions.

Practical 12
Answers to questions
1. Concentrated sulfuric acid.
2. Phosphoric acid and cyclohexanol.
3. Water.
4. $C_6H_{10} + Br_2 \rightarrow C_6H_{10}Br_2$
5. Heat with ethanolic potassium hydroxide.

Practical 13
Answers to questions
1. O_2 from the air oxidises the ethanol to ethanoic acid.
2. **a** propanoic acid
   b pentanoic acid
3. Propan-2-ol oxidises to propanone because the C=O group does not have a C–H bond to oxidise to COOH. Primary alcohols oxidise to aldehydes, which oxidise to carboxylic acids.
   Tertiary alcohols do not oxidise.
4. Some of the ethanol may not have reacted or it may only have reacted as far as ethanal (the aldehyde). Both these substances, as well as water, have boiling points lower than ethanoic acid (carboxylic acid) so they will distil over before the ethanoic acid.
5. Fractional distillation.

Practical 14
Sample data
The time taken for the precipitate to become dense enough to block out the cross is:

1-iodobutane – a few seconds

1-bromobutane – 9 minutes

1-chlorobutane – 20 minutes or more to go slightly cloudy

Rate order:

iodo- > bromo- > chloro-

Answers to questions
1. chloro- > bromo- > iodo-
2. iodo- > bromo- > chloro-
3. The experimental order matches the answer to question 2, so the bond enthalpy must be the more important factor.
4. There might not be the same number of moles of haloalkane in each drop. To make this a fair test, the same number of moles of haloalkane should be used in each reaction.

Practical 15
Sample data

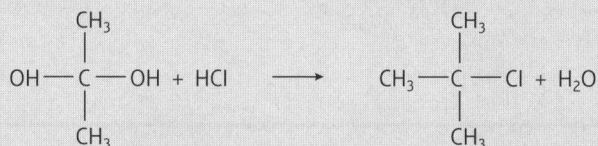

$$OH-\underset{\underset{CH_3}{|}}{\overset{\overset{CH_3}{|}}{C}}-OH + HCl \longrightarrow CH_3-\underset{\underset{CH_3}{|}}{\overset{\overset{CH_3}{|}}{C}}-Cl + H_2O$$

2-methylpropan-2-ol   *2-chloro-2-methylpropane*

The expected yield of the haloalkane would be 3.125 g, when starting with 2.5 g of 2-methylpropan-2-ol.

Your yields are likely to be much lower than this due to incomplete reaction, unwanted products, and loss of product during the purification process.

Answers to questions
1. Unreacted 2-methylpropan-2-ol, other reactants and unwanted products.
2. Hydrochloric acid.
3. Carbon dioxide gas is released as the hydrogencarbonate neutralises the acid.
4. The hydroxide might substitute the halide ion, reversing the reaction.
5. If the liquid boils over a close range and at the expected value, the product must be 2-chloro-2-methylpropane and reasonably pure.
6. Not all the reactants reacted; loss of product during the purification process; unwanted products may have formed.

Practical 16
Analysis of results
Based on these theoretical values, the value for the zinc half-cell is $E^\ominus$ [Zn^{2+}(aq) | Zn(s)] = –0.76 V.

Answers to questions
1. Expected results: $E^\ominus$ [Fe^{2+}(aq) | Fe(s)] and [Cu^{2+}(aq) | Cu(s)] = 0.78 V (your own result may differ)

   $E^\ominus{}_{cell} = E^\ominus{}_{right\text{-}hand\ half\text{-}cell} - E^\ominus{}_{left\text{-}hand\ half\text{-}cell}$

   $0.78 = 0.34 - E^\ominus$ [Fe^{2+}(aq) | Fe(s)]

   The value for the iron half-cell is –0.44 V (or your own result).
2. The experiment was not carried out under standard conditions. In particular, the temperature is not 298 K (cell voltage changes with temperature).
3. Silver nitrate is highly oxidising. An alternative answer is that silver nitrate is very expensive.
4. Magnesium reacts slowly with the water in the solution, raising the concentration of magnesium ions. The equilibrium will move to oppose this change and form more magnesium atoms.

Practical 17
Analysis of results

	Rough	1	2	3	4
Initial reading/cm³					
Final reading/cm³					
Titre/ cm³					

A suitable table is shown above.

Titre values should be recorded to 2 decimal places, with the second figure being 0 or 5 only.

Answers to questions
1. $5Fe^{2+} + MnO_4^- + 8H^+ \rightarrow 5Fe^{3+} + Mn^{2+} + 4H_2O$
2. The answer will depend on your results. If average titre = $21.40\ cm^3$

   $moles = concentration \times \dfrac{volume}{1000}$

   $moles = 0.005 \times \dfrac{21.40}{1000} = 0.000\,107$

   moles of $MnO_4^- = 0.000\,107$
3. Moles of iron = 0.000 535
4. Moles of iron in the 250 cm³ graduated flask = 0.005 35
5. 0.005 35 moles = 0.3 g (or 300 mg in 5 tablets or 60 mg in 1 tablet)
6. The answer will depend on your results, but generally the published result for an iron tablet is 65 mg of iron per tablet.
7. Procedural errors:
   - Stirring may not be sufficient to ensure that all the iron dissolves – warming the solution may help.
   - Transfer of the solution and filtering – ensure that the beaker and the filter paper are rinsed with water.
   - Solution may not be mixed – invert the volumetric flask several times to ensure thorough mixing.
   - Glassware measurements may not be read accurately – read glassware marks from the bottom of the meniscus.
   - End-point may not be clear – use a white tile so that the end-point can be seen clearly.
8. A burette has a margin of error of 0.05 cm³ but as two volume measurements must be subtracted the total uncertainty is 0.1 cm³.

   $(0.1/21.40) \times 100 = 0.46\%$ (The answer will depend on your result for the average titre.)

Practical 18
Analysis of results
- Both graphs of rate against concentration should produce straight lines with positive gradients that pass through the origin.
- The rate with respect to iodide ions is first order.
- The rate with respect to persulfate ions is first order.

Answers to questions

1 One source of procedural error is misjudging the appearance of the blue colour in the solution, i.e. the time at which the colour change occurs.

Another arises from the addition of the starch, which increases the total volume of the mixture slightly.

Measurement uncertainties can occur in measuring the volumes of solution.

For a 2 cm^3 volume measured with a 10 cm^3 measuring cylinder where the smallest scale division is 0.1 cm^3, the measurement uncertainty is ± 0.1 cm^3

% error = $\frac{0.2}{2}$ × 100 = 10%

For a 10 cm^3 volume measured with the same measuring cylinder, the measurement uncertainty is still ± 0.1 cm^3

% error = $\frac{0.2}{10}$ × 100 = 2%

2 The procedural errors are difficult to overcome. One change is to have two students timing simultaneously and using the average value.

Uncertainties in the volume measurements can be minimised by using a more precise measuring instrument, such as a graduated pipette or a burette.

3 Rate = $k[S_2O_8{}^{2-}][I^-]$

4 Step 1 is the rate-determining step. The rate of the reaction is second order and involves one persulfate ion and one iodide ion.

Practical 19
Answers to questions

1 The hydroxyl group

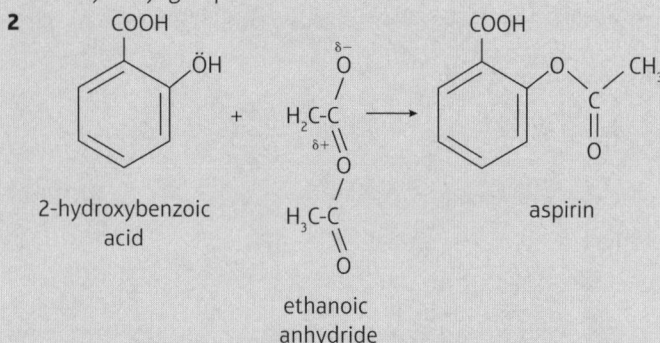

2

2-hydroxybenzoic acid + ethanoic anhydride → aspirin

3 2-hydroxybenzoic acid = 138 and aspirin = 180

4 2.6 g

5 This is dependent on your own results; for 2.1 g of aspirin, percentage yield = 81%

6 Because of impurities in the sample; the crystals may not be dry.

7 Product lost in transfers from one piece of equipment to another, e.g. solid left behind when transferred from weighing scales to flask, liquid left behind on the sides of the reaction flask, small amount of solid left behind on filter paper (not scraped off); some product remains in solution (filtrate).

8 Filtration is fast and solid will be almost dry.

9 Unreacted 2-hydroxybenzoic acid.

10 You should record a melting point range rather than a single temperature. This is because impurities in the sample cause the solid to melt over a temperature range, rather than sharply at one temperature. The narrower the range and the closer your value to 136 °C, the purer the sample.

Practical 20
Answers to questions

1 Answers will depend on your results. For the sample data given, the enthalpy changes of solution are:

−28.2 kJ mol^{-1} for LiCl

+4.2 kJ mol^{-1} for NaCl

+16.7 kJ mol^{-1} for KCl

2 Enthalpies of solution become more endothermic (increase) going down the group.

enthalpy change of solution = enthalpy of hydration − lattice enthalpy

At the top of the group, where ionic radius is small, the enthalpy of hydration is more exothermic than the lattice enthalpy.

3 Any answer between +24 and +30 kJ mol^{-1}

4 −849 − 28.2 = x + (−384.1)

x = −493.1 kJ mol^{-1} (for the data above)

5 Errors can arise:
- if not all the solid is transferred from the weighing boat as it is difficult to see if the solid has dissolved
- errors for a measuring cylinder = $\frac{1}{50}$ × 100 = 2%
- errors for a thermometer = $\frac{0.5}{13}$ × 100 = 3.8%

6 Weighing the weighing boat after the solid has been added. Using a more accurate thermometer (× 0.1 °C) or a datalogger and a temperature probe.

Practical 21
Answers to questions

1 The chloride ion, Cl$^-$

$[Cu(H_2O)_6]^{2+}(aq) + 4Cl^-(aq) \rightarrow [CuCl_4]^{2-}(aq) + 6H_2O(l)$

2 The ammonia molecule, NH$_3$

$[Cu(H_2O)_6]^{2+}(aq) + 4NH_3(aq) \rightarrow [Cu(NH_3)_4(H_2O)_2]^{2+}(aq) + 4H_2O(l)$

3 The chloride ion

$[Co(H_2O)_6]^{2+}(aq) + 4Cl^-(aq) \rightarrow [CoCl_4]^{2-}(aq) + 6H_2O(l)$

4 The chloride ion is replaced by ammonia and water.

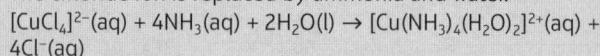

$[CuCl_4]^{2-}(aq) + 4NH_3(aq) + 2H_2O(l) \rightarrow [Cu(NH_3)_4(H_2O)_2]^{2+}(aq) + 4Cl^-(aq)$

5 $[Cu(H_2O)_6]^{2+}(aq) < [CuCl_4]^{2-}(aq) < [Cu(NH_3)_4(H_2O)_2]^{2+}(aq)$

The chloride replaced the water readily when hydrochloric acid was added to the copper(II) solution. In turn, the ammonia replaced the chloride ions readily when ammonia was added to the copper(II)/chloride ion complex.

6 Yes. A high value for the stability constant indicates a stable complex. The value for the copper(II)/ammonia complex is much higher than that for the copper(II)/chloride complex.

Practical 22
Analysis of results

1 The product of the reaction between a carbonyl compound and 2,4-DNPH is a yellow/orange crystalline solid.

2 X is benzaldehyde, Y is propanone, Z is propanal.

Answers to questions

1 A condensation reaction.

2 The product is recrystallised to remove any impurities; any remaining impurity will lower the melting point.

3 A hot solvent is used so that the solvent is saturated with the solute. If you add more than the minimum volume of hot solvent to dissolve a solid during recrystallisation then too much solid will remain in solution on cooling and will be lost, resulting in a low yield.

4 Any water/ethanol still present will behave as an impurity; this will lower the melting point.

5 Infrared spectroscopy; mass spectrometry; NMR

6 **Infrared spectroscopy**

The spectrum will have an absorption at 1680–1750 cm^{-1}, showing the presence of the carbonyl group (or C=O bond).

Mass spectrometry

The molecular ion peak (furthest to the right) will give the relative molecular mass of the compound. Fragmentation will also produce ions that include the carbonyl group because they are relatively stable.

NMR

The different proton environments can be identified from the chemical shifts of the peaks. The relative areas under the peaks will give the relative number of protons present in each. Any splitting patterns observed will give the number of protons in the adjacent environment (according to the $n + 1$ rule).

Practical 23

Titre values should be recorded to 2 decimal places, with the second figure being 0 or 5 only.

The graph produced should be a straight line with a negative gradient: the rate of reaction is constant no matter what the concentration of the reactant is.

Hence the graph produced should show that the reaction is zero order with respect to iodine.

Answers to questions

1 The rate doubles.
2 The rate doubles.
3 The rate remains the same.
4 Rate = $k[H^+][CH_3COCH_3]$
5 The graph would be a curve. To prove that the reaction is first order, you can look at the half-life at various points – the half-life will be constant for a first order reaction. Alternatively plot a graph of rate against concentration. For a first order reaction, this will be a straight-line graph as shown in Figure B.

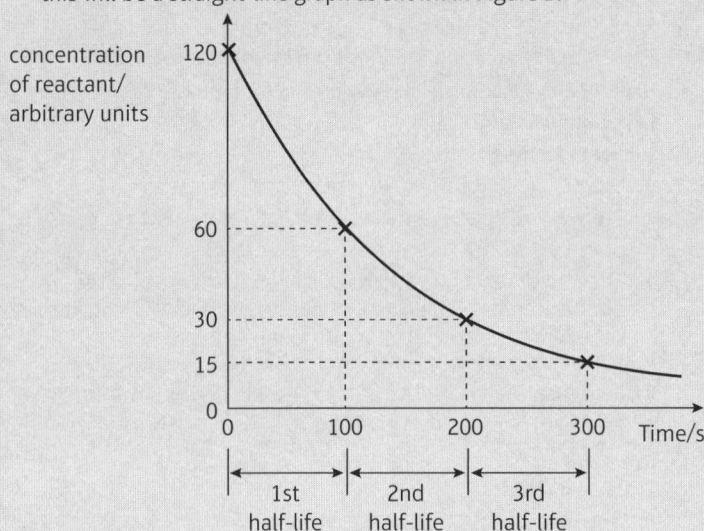

Figure A. A graph of concentration of reactant against time for a first order reaction.

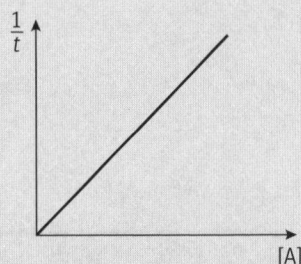

Figure B. A graph of rate against concentration for a first order reaction

Practical 24
Sample data

R_f values for this solvent are:

glycine = 0.26
leucine = 0.73
proline = 0.43
serine = 0.27
valine = 0.60

Answers to questions

1 Amino acids are colourless in solution, so the spots in a chromatogram are also colourless. They must be stained by spraying them with ninhydrin to produce coloured spots.
2 The solute molecules would dissolve in the solvent and the chromatogram would be blank.
3 Paper chromatography: stationary phase is the water held in the paper; mobile phase is the solvent.
   TLC: stationary phase is the silica; mobile phase is the solvent.

4 The solute moves up the paper by partition between the water (in the paper) and the solvent. During TLC, the process on the slide is adsorption if the silica is completely dry. If it has absorbed water from the air then both adsorption and partition can happen together.
5 The lid helps the atmosphere in the container become saturated with solvent vapour so the equilibrium that happens in partition can be established more quickly.
6 TLC is quicker; smaller quantities of solute can be used.

Practical 25
Analysis of results

- mass of 3 cm³ of methyl benzoate = 3.27 g
- 100% conversion would produce 2.93 g of benzoic acid
- melting point of benzoic acid is 122 °C.

Answers to questions

1 To allow time for the reaction to be completed and to prevent the escape of volatile liquids (any volatile liquids condense and return to the reaction flask so no products will be lost).
2 Alkaline hydrolysis of an ester produces the carboxylate. The solution was acidified to convert the carboxylate into the carboxylic acid.
3 The polarity of the bonds in the COOH group in ethanoic acid produces interactions with polar water molecules; as well as dipole–dipole interactions, there will be hydrogen bonding between the acid and the water. The large benzene ring in benzoic acid is non-polar. The delocalised π-electrons are attracted to the carbon atoms in the COOH groups, which reduces the polarity of the bonds. This means that the intermolecular interactions and the solubility of benzoic acid in cold water are also reduced.
4 So that the solvent is saturated with the solute; this maximises the yield.
5 When the impure solid is dissolved in the solvent, soluble impurities stay in solution because different substances have different solubilities in the solvent. The impure substance crystallises before the impurities.
6 The volume of methyl benzoate is measured in a 10 cm³ measuring cylinder; because the yield is based on this measurement it would be more appropriate to measure it in a graduated pipette.
7 The methyl benzoate may not be completely hydrolysed when it is refluxed; some of the product is lost during each step of the purification process.

Practical 26
Sample data

T/°C	Time/s	T/K	1/T/K⁻¹	ln t
15	440	288	0.00347	6.1
25	221	298	0.00336	5.4
35	90	308	0.00325	4.5
45	45	318	0.00314	3.8
55	20	328	0.00305	3.0
65	8	338	0.00296	2.1
75	4	348	0.00278	1.4

Gradient of the graph = 6816

E_a = gradient × R = 56 676 J mol⁻¹

Answers to questions

1 $C_6H_5OH + 3Br_2 \rightarrow C_6H_2Br_3OH + 3HBr$
2 When all the phenol has reacted, the bromine continuously produced in the first reaction will then react with the methyl red indicator, bleaching its colour.
3 This will depend on your data but using the sample data the answer should be approximately 6816.
4 E_a = 56 668 to 56 676 J mol⁻¹ approximately

Practical 27
Sample data

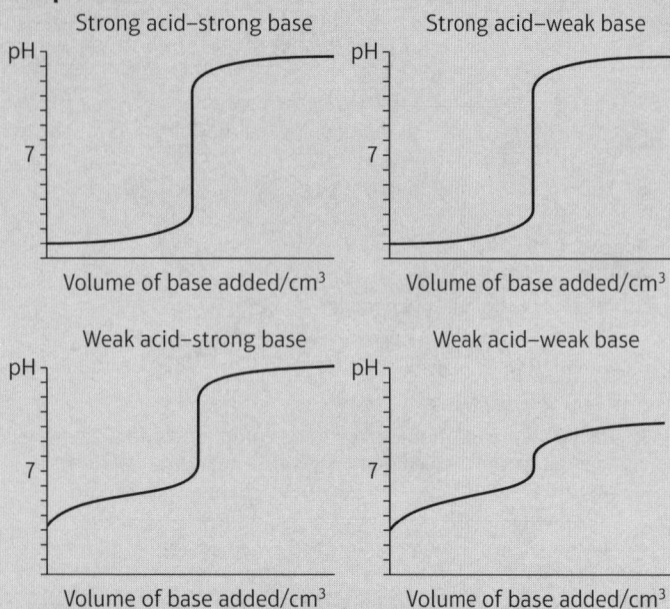

Strong acid–strong base

Strong acid–weak base

Weak acid–strong base

Weak acid–weak base

Answers to questions

1 $HCl + NaOH \rightarrow NaCl + H_2O$; strong acid–strong base
   $HCl + NH_3 \rightarrow NH_4Cl$; strong acid–weak base
   $CH_3COOH + NaOH \rightarrow CH_3COO^-Na^+ + H_2O$; weak acid–strong base
   $CH_3COOH + NH_3 \rightarrow CH_3COO^-NH_4^+$; weak acid–weak base

2 SA–SB   pH 4–10
   SA–WB   pH 4–8
   WA–SB   pH 6–10
   WA–WB   pH 6.5–7.5

3 SA–SB: any indicator that changes colour between 4 and 10.
   SA–WB: any indicator that changes colour between 4 and 8.
   WA–SB: any indicator that changes colour between 6 and 10.
   WA–WB: bromothymol blue.

4 The curve rises steadily from beginning to end; there is no steep rise around equivalence as in the other three curves.

5 $pH = -\log(0.15) = 0.82$

6 The curve should begin at pH = 0.82; when the volume of base is 0 cm^3. There should be a steep rise in the curve between pH 4 and pH 8 when the reading on the x-axis is 20 cm^3. The curve should finish at pH 9 when the volume of added base is 25 cm^3.

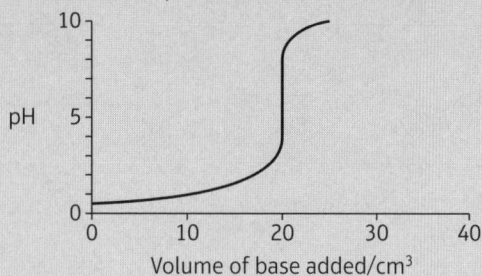

Practical 28
Analysis of results

Titre values should be recorded to 2 decimal places with the second figure being 0 or 5 only.

The titration should be repeated until concordant results are obtained.

Answers to questions

1 This answer will depend on your own findings but the pH should be 4.77. In this case, $[H^+] = 1.7 \times 10^{-5}$ mol dm^{-3}.

2 1.7×10^{-5} mol dm^{-3}

3 Parallax error in taking burette readings; error in counting unmarked graduation marks on the burette; and difficulty identifying the exact end-point. Read glassware from the bottom of the meniscus; use a white tile so you can see the colour change clearly.

Practical 29
Expected results

Experiment 1: pH 2–3.

Experiment 2: hydrogen is produced, gas pops with a lighted splint.

Experiment 3: solution is neutralised by sodium hydroxide.

Experiment 4: carbon dioxide is produced, limewater turns milky.

Experiment 5: smell of pear drops (ester).

Answers to questions

1 Step 2: $2CH_3COOH + Mg \rightarrow (CH_3COO)_2Mg + H_2$
   Step 3: $CH_3COOH + NaOH \rightarrow CH_3COO^-Na^+ + H_2O$
   Step 4: $2CH_3COOH + Na_2CO_3 \rightarrow 2CH_3COO^-Na^+ + H_2O + CO_2$

2 The rate of reaction with magnesium is not vigorous; the effervescence will be slow and the magnesium will not dissolve quickly. The pH will be between 3 and 4. The reaction with sodium carbonate will be slow.

3 Esterification or condensation; $CH_3COOH + C_2H_5OH \rightarrow CH_3COOC_2H_5 + H_2O$

Practical 30
Expected results

A: copper carbonate

B: sodium sulfate

C: calcium bromide

D: iron chloride

X: cyclohexene

Y: propanal

Z: ethanoic acid

Answers to questions

1 It removes anions such as carbonate ions, which would form a precipitate with silver nitrate.

2 Add dilute hydrochloric acid: sulfate(IV) ions will dissolve but sulfate(VI) ions will not.

3 Heat with Fehling's or Benedict's solution; the formation of a red precipitate indicates the presence of an aldehyde group.

Practical 1

- $\text{moles} = \dfrac{\text{mass}}{M_r}$

Practical 2

- Write balanced equations.

Practical 3

- Calculate relative atomic mass.

Practical 4

- $\text{moles} = \text{concentration} \times \dfrac{\text{volume (cm}^3)}{1000}$

- $\text{moles} = \dfrac{\text{mass}}{M_r}$

Practical 6

- Write balanced equations.

Practical 7

- Plot a graph.
- Substitute numerical values into algebraic equations using appropriate units for physical quantities.

Practical 8

- Plot a graph.
- Draw tangents.
- Calculate measurement errors.

Practical 9

- Find arithmetic means.
- Plot data on a graph.

Practical 10

- Calculate concentrations of reagents.

Practical 11

- Understand and use the symbol $\rightleftharpoons$.

Practical 12

- Write a balanced equation.
- Calculate percentage mass and empirical formulae.

Practical 13

- Balance equations.

Practical 15

- Calculate numbers of moles.
- Balance equations.

Practical 16

- Substitute numerical values into algebraic equations using appropriate units for physical quantities.
- Calculation of a standard cell potential by combining two standard electrode potentials:

  $E^{\ominus}_{\text{cell}} = E^{\ominus}_{\text{right-hand half-cell}} - E^{\ominus}_{\text{left-hand half-cell}}$

Practical 17

- Change the subject of an equation.
- Substitute numerical values into algebraic equations using appropriate units for physical quantities.
- Use an appropriate number of significant figures.
- Identify uncertainties in measurements and use simple techniques to determine uncertainty when data are combined.

Practical 18

- Translate information between graphical, numerical and algebraic forms.
- Plot two variables from experimental or other data.
- Use an appropriate number of significant figures.
- Identify uncertainties in measurements and use simple techniques to determine uncertainty when data are combined.

Practical 19

- Substitute numerical values into algebraic equations using appropriate units for physical quantities.
- Use ratios, fractions and percentages.
- Use an appropriate number of significant figures.

Practical 20

- Substitute numerical values into algebraic equations using appropriate units for physical quantities.
- Use an appropriate number of significant figures.

Practical 21

- Translate information between graphical, numerical and algebraic forms.

Practical 23

- Calculate a rate of change from a graph showing a linear relationship.
- Plot two variables from experimental or other data.

Practical 24

- Recognise and make use of appropriate units in calculations.

Practical 25

- Substitute numerical values into algebraic equations using appropriate units for physical quantities.
- Use ratios, fractions and percentages.
- Use an appropriate number of significant figures.

Practical 26

- Use a calculator to find and use exponential and logarithmic functions.
- Substitute numerical values into algebraic equations using appropriate units for physical quantities.
- Plot two variables from experimental or other data.
- Determine the slope and intercept of a linear graph.
- Use an appropriate number of significant figures.

Practical 27

- Use calculators to find and use power, exponential and logarithmic functions.
- Use logarithms in relation to quantities that range over several orders of magnitude.
- Plot two variables from experimental or other data.

Practical 28

- Use calculators to find and use power, exponential and logarithmic functions.
- Use an appropriate number of significant figures.
- Use logarithms in relation to quantities that range over several orders of magnitude.
- Change the subject of an equation.
- Substitute numerical values into algebraic equations using appropriate units for physical quantities.

Students should use this space for any rough notes, diagrams or calculations.

Students should use this space for any rough notes, diagrams or calculations.

Students should use this space for any rough notes, diagrams or calculations.

Student Notes

Students should use this space for any rough notes, diagrams or calculations.

We have attempted to identify all the recognised hazards in the practical activities in this guide. The Activity and Assessment Pack provides suitable warnings about the hazards and suggests appropriate precautions. Teachers and technicians should remember, however, that where there is a hazard, the employer is required to carry out a risk assessment under either the COSHH Regulations or the Management of Health and Safety at Work Regulations. Most education employers have adopted a range of nationally available publications as model (general) risk assessments and, where such published assessments exist for the activity, our advice is believed to be compatible with them.

We have assumed that practical work is carried out in a properly equipped and maintained laboratory and that any fieldwork takes account of the employer's guidelines. In particular, we have assumed that any mains-operated electrical equipment is properly maintained, that students have been shown how to conduct normal laboratory operations (such as heating or handling heavy objects) safely and that good practice is observed when chemicals or living organisms are handled (see below). We have also assumed that classes are sufficiently small and well-behaved for a teacher to be able to exercise adequate supervision of the students and that rooms are not so crowded that students' activities pose a danger to their neighbours.

CLEAPSS School Science Service are reviewing but not trialling this text. Following receipt of the CLEAPPS review any such guidance on how to make this resource conform to the above policy will be incorporated and the resources updated.

Important note

Neither Pearson, the authors nor the series editor take responsibility for the safety of any activity. Before doing any practical activity you are legally required to carry out your own risk assessment. In particular, any local rules issued by your employer must be obeyed, regardless of what is recommended in this resource. Where students are required to write their own risk assessments they must always be checked by the teacher and revised, as necessary, to cover any issues the students may have overlooked. The teacher should always have the final control as to how the practical is conducted.

Further sources of information: CLEAPSS, www.cleapss.org.uk (includes Secondary Science Laboratory Handbook and Hazcards)